Gemmology

Love, joy and peace
to you, my darling
Iris, at Christmas
and always.

Yours aye,
Sandie

1971

Other titles in preparation

Birds

Flowers

Gemmology

John Sweeney

Longman

Longman Rhodesia (Pvt) Ltd
Beatrice Road, Southerton, Salisbury

*Associated companies, branches and
representatives throughout the world*

© J. W. Sweeney and SCNVYO

First published 1971

ISBN 0 582 64104 7

Printed in Rhodesia by Mardon Printers (Pvt) Limited, Salisbury

Contents

Acknowledgement

To my wife Deirdre, who over the years watched my collection of specimens and stones grow until they filled every nook and cranny of our house. There was no complaint; indeed, she always encouraged me in this all-absorbing hobby.

My sincere thanks go to Maureen Laming who gave up much of her valuable spare time to type the script, to Arthur Niven who also gave up his spare time to do all the line drawings and, last but not least, Ray Venter who spent hours of daylight during his weekends to produce all the photographs which have been included in the book.

Author's Note

This book has been written with the object of interesting the public in the absorbing hobby of gem and mineral study, collecting specimens and cutting gemstones. For those enthusiasts who are already members of gem and mineral societies or are rockhounds of some standing, this note will contain nothing new, but for the beginner it is a word of warning before he suddenly finds that he has broken the law.

1. No person is allowed to prospect in Rhodesia unless he is the holder of a valid prospecting licence.
2. No person is allowed to prospect on privately owned land until he has advised the owner of the land of his intention.
3. No person may remove any mineral from a prospect except for testing purposes or with the permission of the Mining Commissioner.
4. A considerable portion of all privately owned land is closed to prospecting because the owner has developed it in one way or another: ensure that these categories are well known.
5. Mining Commissioners are stationed in Bulawayo, Fort Victoria, Gatooma, Gwelo and Salisbury and, if the rockhound is in any doubt regarding his rights to prospect in certain areas, he should consult the Mining Commissioner before embarking on a field trip. This will not only save considerable time, but will also assist the rockhound in keeping on the right side of the law.
6. The mining laws of Rhodesia have been drawn up to protect the miner and prospector as well as the landowner and it is only by observing them fully that the prospector can enjoy to the full the privileges granted to the holder of a prospecting licence.

Introduction

As far back as man can remember, gemstones have been a source of joy and pleasure to the human race. Gems have always been used as a means of adornment, both from the artistic and religious angles, as a source of exchange in the early days of trading and as tokens of good or bad luck.

Some of the earliest written references to gemstones are contained in the Old Testament where mention is made in Exodus of the breastplate made for Aaron, the high priest.

Biblical and lapidary researchers have spent many years in an effort to reach agreement on the various stones which were included in the breastplate which appears to have been made in or about 1250 B.C. There are still several conflicting theories regarding the type of stones used in the breastplate, because the ancient Hebrews used to refer to stones either by colour or sparkle and many authorities were of the opinion that the ancient Hebrew would have been unable to cut and shape any stone which was harder than quartz. However, after considerable investigation, most people are now of the opinion that the following stones which represent the twelve tribes of Israel must have been used:

> Red jasper
> Citrine
> Emerald
> Ruby
> Lapis lazuli
> Rock crystal
> Golden sapphire
> Blue sapphire
> Amethyst
> Yellow jasper
> Golden beryl and
> Chrysoprase.

It is interesting to note that, with the exception of lapis lazuli, all the stones mentioned have been mined in Rhodesia.

Over the years certain gemstones have, in addition to the earlier religious associations, gradually assumed mystical and superstitious connections as well. For example, the opal is considered to be an unlucky stone if worn by anyone who is not born in October or under the sign of Libra. The Hope diamond is also reputed to be unlucky and is supposed to bring bad luck and disaster to anyone who owns it.

There may or may not be any truth in these associations, but in a similar vein and on a lighter note, certain stones are supposed to bring good luck to people born in certain months and over the years the following list of birthstones has been evolved:

January	garnet or rose quartz
February	amethyst or onyx
March	bloodstone or aquamarine
April	diamond or rock crystal
May	emerald or chrysoprase
June	pearl, alexandrite or moonstone
July	ruby or carnelian
August	sardonyx, peridot or aventurine
September	sapphire or lapis lazuli
October	opal or tourmaline
November	topaz or citrine
December	turquoise or zircon

The ancient Romans believed that the amethyst was a guard against drunkenness and the stone in any form was therefore much sought after by the lords and ladies of the time. If there were any truth in this theory, however, the amethyst would doubtless still be in demand. The ancient Romans also believed that the diamond played a significant part in moulding the future of any love affair. They started the tradition of giving wives and sweethearts diamonds to prove their affection, loyalty and honest intentions. This tradition has persisted and modern man still gives a diamond ring to confirm his engagement.

Many tales are told about gemstones, their beauty or their supernatural powers, but the most significant thing about them is the value which has been attached to the intrinsically valueless material of which they are formed. Over the years men have committed murder for the sake of gems, they have stolen and cheated in order to possess them and, when the value of money appeared to be on the decline, put their all into the bright little gems. When everything else seemed lost, gems have managed to maintain their value and in many cases the value has actually increased. This state of affairs has been most noticeable during the past two decades because the value of good gems has been appreciating at the rate of between ten per cent and fifteen per cent per annum, a rate which far exceeds the depreciating value of money.

What is a Gemstone?

There are many beautiful minerals locked up in the earth, a vast number of which are of academic interest only to the pure gemmologist. These stones may be of interest to the specimen collector, but the average man in the street only knows of them because of the minerals which they contain. What then is it that is responsible for the raising of one stone to the exclusive position of 'gemstone' while another apparently equally beautiful and attractive stone is relegated for ever to the classification of 'mineral'?

Several important factors are responsible for division between the two groups and this may be an opportune time to examine a few of the more obvious ones.

Hardness

This is possibly the most important factor governing the classification of 'gemstone'. Any gemstone must be hard enough and sufficiently compact to take a good polish and having once taken it, must be hard enough to retain it in spite of constant use. Generally speaking, a ring stone which is subjected to bumps and knocks, must have a hardness at least equal to the hardness of the dust which settles on the furniture. Dust, as everyone knows, contains a fairly high percentage of silica which has the same hardness as quartz. It therefore stands to reason that any stone which is softer than quartz will, if constantly knocked against tables and chairs which have small grains of silica adhering to them, soon become scratched and dull and lose its beauty. Gemmologists are consequently of the opinion that true gemstones can only be those stones which fall within the hardness bracket from quartz up to diamond, the hardest known stone.

There are exceptions to almost every rule and this is also the case where hardness of gemstones is concerned. The precious opal of South Australia and the fire opal of Mexico are both considerably softer than quartz. Nevertheless, both these stones make up in sheer beauty and lustre what they lack in hardness and are readily accepted by everyone as true gemstones. Another minor departure from the general rule is that items of jewellery, such as brooches and necklaces, are frequently made of stones softer than quartz, because they do not receive the same rough treatment which is meted out to ring stones and are therefore able to retain their polish.

Lustre and brilliance

Hardness alone cannot make a gemstone: thus an industrial diamond which is dull and lustreless cannot, by any stretch of the imagination, be classed as a gemstone. Lustre and brilliance are terms used by gemmologists to describe the effect produced when light rays are reflected from the surface of a polished object.

For example, the characteristically high lustre of a diamond or a sphene or a zircon is referred to as 'adamantine', while the glassy appearance of aquamarine, emeralds, quartz, rubies and sapphires is known as 'vitreous'. Chalcedony and jade, on the other hand, have a distinctly 'fatty' or 'waxy' lustre and haematite, gold and silver have a 'metallic' lustre.

Colour

Perhaps more so today than at any other time, colour plays a most important part in the popularity of a gemstone. A brown topaz or zircon is not as popular as a good blue aquamarine. Yet a blue or golden topaz or a green or red zircon will always be more highly prized than an aquamarine of the same size. Fashion too plays a fairly big part in the colour scheme. Today, the western world prizes green above all other coloured stones, while in the east, red stones are in the greatest demand.

Scarcity

Scarcity and rareness are important factors controlling the value of gemstones. This explains the value and popularity of diamonds, emeralds, rubies and sapphires. Those stones for which the demand will always exceed the supply must remain the most valuable and sought after. Scarcity can, however, have the opposite effect as well. For instance, a stone which is so rare as to be almost unknown, cannot be as popular to the man in the street as a well known yet possibly less attractive stone.

Use of correct names

Over the ages gemstones have been known by a variety of different names; in the past this was due to a large extent to ignorance. For example, red garnets and rubies were considered to be the same stone and were lumped together under the common name 'carbuncle'. Today, however, with all our improved methods of determining the various minerals, there is no excuse for giving a particular stone the wrong name. The various trade names and other misleading names, which are frequently given to stones to dupe a gullible public into buying a cheap stone under the mistaken impression that it is something better, is nothing short of criminal.

For this reason in many parts of the world today we find that laws have been introduced which prohibit the use of incorrect names unless the accepted name is also shown. If similar laws were enforced on a world-wide basis much of the hard-earned money which is being wasted on rubbish today could be saved for better things.

To assist readers in determining what they are buying, a short list is given below showing the correct and accepted names against the incorrect names:

INCORRECT NAME	CORRECT NAME
African or Transvaal jade	grossularite garnet
Cape ruby	pyrope garnet
Oriental emerald	green sapphire
Brazilian emerald	green tourmaline
Balas ruby	red spinel
Oriental jade	serpentine or soapstone
American diamond	rock crystal (quartz)
Madeira topaz	citrine or burnt amethyst
Smoky topaz	smoky quartz
Rhodesian moonstone	milky quartz

In addition to the above there are several minerals which have been given trade names, which, although not misleading and now accepted by the public, do not convey the true mineral content of the stone: an example of this is 'unakite'—a combination of feldspar and epidote and mtorolite—a chrome-coloured chalcedony located only in Rhodesia.

While on the subject of correct nomenclature, it is worth mentioning that the public can be misled in other ways as well.

The stones displayed in shop windows can be divided into four main groups, i.e.

1. *Natural stones*   those made by nature and dug out of the ground by the miner
2. *Altered stones*   stones usually of natural origin treated or dyed to give them the appearance of being something else
3. *Synthetic stones*   those stones, usually corundum or spinel, which are made by man from the same ingredients that nature used when forming her stones
4. *Imitation stones*   usually made of glass or paste with the addition of colouring matter.

In the first group we find all our true gemstones in their natural colours. In the second group we find many of the altered stones which are used to deceive the public: stones such as amethyst, which, when heat treated, turn a beautiful golden brown and are sold as topaz or Madeira topaz, and chalcedony and agate which have been dyed chemically but are still sold as the natural stone. In this group we also find pale green or white beryls which have been subjected to a bombardment of chromium atoms—treatment which gives the stones the appearance of emeralds of superb quality and they are sometimes sold as such.

The third group is made up of man-made stones containing the natural elements, together with colouring matter, and almost every known stone can be copied, if not in its true chemical constituents, at least in colour. The two main stones in this group are, as previously stated, corundum and spinel, but synthetic emeralds are becoming fairly common and it is possible that synthetic diamonds of gem quality may shortly appear on the market.

The fourth group, which is made of glass, paste or nylon is more readily distinguishable, because the colour is seldom true and the specific gravity is invariably incorrect. It should also be noted that the colour is usually too vivid although the stone nevertheless lacks lustre.

Testing Gemstones

In the following pages we will take a brief look at some of the more important yet often simple tests which can be made in order to determine the exact nature of any gemstone. With experience, most people who are interested in gemmology will be able to tell the difference between, for example, a beryl crystal and a garnet crystal. This is because they are different in colour and belong to different crystallographic systems. This method of determining various materials is very basic and in many cases may prove adequate, but in every rockhound's life the occasion must arise when the basic tests of shape and colour are insufficient and it becomes necessary to carry out more extensive tests in order to determine the exact nature of the material.

Testing materials in a geological laboratory can be a very tedious and long-winded business involving the use of highly complicated and expensive equipment such as dichroscopes, microscopes and spectroscopes, just to mention a few items. It is, however, most unlikely that amateurs will possess anything like the full range of testing equipment and information contained in this chapter will deal only with the simpler methods which can be employed. *It is essential, however, that the reader remembers that the tests and methods outlined here can never be taken as conclusive evidence that an unusual stone or crystal is what it appears to be and if there is any doubt in the rockhound's mind he must not hesitate to take the material to someone who is better qualified and better able to determine the exact nature of the stone.* This will not only give the amateur the opportunity to test his skill and ability but will also ensure that he does not treat what might be a valuable specimen as just another lump of quartz.

Crystallography

Most minerals have a basic crystalline form. This is not, however, always apparent, possibly because the crystals are too small to be seen with the naked eye or because the mineral growth has been restricted or interfered with by the surrounding rocks. The best crystals are therefore those which have been allowed by nature to grow in rock cavities or vugs. The finest examples of these can be seen in the amethyst geodes.

For obvious reasons crystals which are well formed are always in great demand as collectors' pieces and the rockhound should therefore be as careful as possible when extracting crystals because even those which are of no particular interest to the cutter may be of immense interest and value to the collector.

Crystal symmetry is derived from the regular formation of the atoms which comprise a particular mineral, and because the structure of similar stones never varies we can expect the crystal of any particular mineral to follow the same basic form every time.

There are six main crystallographic systems which in turn can be broken down into something like thirty different classes. Many of these classes vary to such a small extent from their neighbours that there is little or no object is attempting to differentiate between all of them and it will be adequate for the purposes of this book to deal solely with the six main systems and a few of the major classes.

Any discussion on crystal structure must include reference to symmetry. A true crystal, that is one that has developed unhindered in any way, must be perfectly symmetrical.

There are three different aspects of symmetry which must be considered in any basic study. These are briefly:

1   *Planes of symmetry*

Any object placed in front of a mirror will produce an image in the mirror which is the exact replica of the object. Therefore, if a perfect crystal is split in half and the half placed in front of the mirror, that half, together with the half image in the mirror, must form the exact replica of the original crystal.

2   *Axes of symmetry*

The axes of symmetry in any perfect crystal are those imaginary lines through the crystal about which the crystal can be rotated and yet continue to show an identical image at any given angle of rotation. A typical example of this is a child's cubic building block, as shown in the diagram on page 10.

Imagine that the lines '*a*', '*b*' and '*c*' are in fact thin rigid wires passing through the block from the exact centre of one plane to the exact centre of the opposite plane. Hold the points of, say, the '*c*' wire between your fingers and rotate the block through 180°; an identical view of the block is obtained. The same would be the case if the block was rotated around either the '*a*' or '*b*' axes. The cube, as will be seen when it is rotated around any of the three axes will present an identical image on

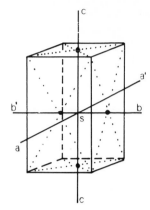

four different occasions if rotated through 90° on each occasion. This is known as four-fold symmetry and is peculiar to the true cube.

3 Centre of symmetry

The centre of symmetry is a point in the exact centre of the crystal through which all the axes must pass. In the diagram above, this centre point has been marked with an '*s*' for easy identification.

Crystallographic axes

Having briefly described the axes of symmetry, it is now possible to proceed with the next step in our study of crystallography. The imaginary lines '*a*', '*b*' and '*c*' are used to define the faces of the crystal, thus the cube or cubic system has, as already indicated, three equal length axes which all interesect at the centre of symmetry at 90° to each other.

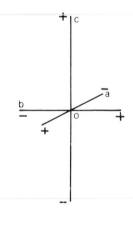

For uniformity the '*c*' axis is always known as the vertical axis and runs through the length of the crystal. In the average crystal this is usually the longest axis. The '*b*' axis on the other hand is always known as the horizontal axis. The axes are always depicted in the manner indicated in the sketch and indicate the faces of the crystal.

THE SIX CRYSTAL SYSTEMS

Cubic	Tetragonal	Hexagonal	Orthorhombic	Monoclinic	Triclinic
ee axes of al length rsecting at ht angles.	*Two equal hori-zontal axes. Vertical axes shorter or longer. All intersecting at right angles.*	*Three equal hor-izontal axes intersect at 120°. Vertical axis per-pendicular to horizontal axis.*	*Three unequal axes intersect at right angles.*	*Three unequal axes. Two intersect at right angles and the other inter-sects at a small-er angle.*	*Three unequal axes. None intersect at right angles.*

II

Crystallographic systems

There are six major crystal groups and all the known crystalline or crystal forming minerals will fall into one or other of these major groups. The various groups are:

1	Cubic system	4	Monoclinic system
2	Tetragonal system	5	Triclinic system
3	Orthorhombic system	6	Hexagonal system

1 *Cubic system*

This is the simplest crystal system. There are three axes all equal in length and all angles, i.e. *c o b*, *a o b* and *a o c* are right angles. Because there is no true vertical axis which is longer than the other two, we can in this instance dispense with *a*, *b* and *c* axes and refer to them all as '*a*' axes. Some well known stones which fall into this category are diamonds, garnets, fluorspar and spinel.

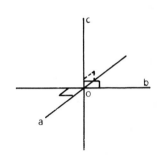

2 *Tetragonal system*

In the tetragonal system the '*c*' or vertical axis is longer than the '*a*' and '*b*' axes which are equal in length to each other. As in the cubic system, however, all angles are right angles.

Some well known stones which fall into this group are zircon and scapolite.

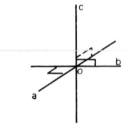

3 *Orthorhombic system*

In the orthorhombic system all axes are different lengths but once again all angles are right angles.

Common minerals which fall into this group are alexandrite, olivine (peridot) and topaz.

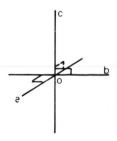

4 Monoclinic system

In the monoclinic system all axes are different in length. The important difference, however, between this system and the orthorhombic system is that while angles $c \, o \, b$ and $b \, o \, a$ are right angles the angle $c \, o \, a$ is not at right angles.

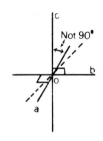

Some common minerals that fall into this group are hornblende, augite, kunzite and feldspar.

5 Triclinic system

In the triclinic system not only are the three axes all of different lengths but all the angles between the axes are also different.

Common minerals which fall into this system are kyanite and albite.

6 Hexagonal system

The hexagonal system is unlike any of the previous five systems in that there is an additional axis 'a'. The angles between the 'c' axis and the other three axes are always right angles while the angles $b \, o \, a$, $a \, o \, a$ and $a \, o \, b$ are always 60°. The 'c' axis is once again the longest while all other axes are equal in length.

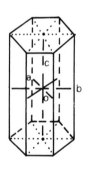

Common minerals in this group are beryl, corundum, quartz and tourmaline.

Optical properties of stones

Refractive index

Refraction or refractive index is one of the most important and conclusive means available for determining the true nature of a gemstone or any other stone which is not opaque. There are several types of instruments known as refractometers which are readily available at fairly reasonable prices. They are used to measure the refractive index and are strongly recommended for this purpose.

A brief explanation of refraction or refractive index at this stage will assist in understanding what actually happens. When a beam of light falls on the surface of a transparent stone, part of the light is reflected from the surface at an angle equal to the angle created by the beam and the surface of the stone, and it is this reflected light which gives the stone its surface lustre. However, by far the greater proportion of the light penetrates the stone, but because of the denser nature of the material as compared with the surrounding air, the velocity at which the light travels is considerably reduced and the new path is nearer the perpendicular or normal.

The following diagram will assist in explaining the position:

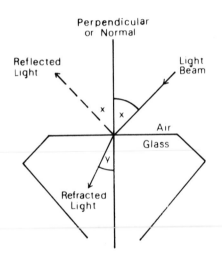

In the diagram the angles 'x' are known as the angles of incidence while the angle 'y' is known as the angle of refraction.

The greater the refractive index of any particular stone, the greater the brilliance of that stone. The actual figures shown in the scale are arrived at not by guesswork, but by a mathematical formula based on the speed of light in the air as opposed to the speed of light in the stone.

The speed of light in space is approximately 300 000 000 metres per second and it has been calculated that the speed of light in diamond is approximately 123 700 000 metres per second. By dividing 300 000 000 by 123 700 000 we arrive at 2·42, the refractive index of the diamond.

In the same way light travels through:

(a)   sapphire at approximately 170 074 000 metres per second giving a refractive index of 1.76

(b)   emerald at approximately 189 447 000 metres per second giving a refractive index of 1·58

(c)   amethyst at approximately 193 117 000 metres per second giving a refractive index of 1·55.

With the majority of gemstones one will see two shadows across the refractometer scale, the darker shadow on the lower number while the lighter shadow will pass through the higher number. Thus with quartz we will see the figures 1·54 and 1·55 indicated by the two shadows. This does not mean that the refractometer is faulty, but that the stone has what is known as 'double refraction'. The refractive index of such stones is shown by two figures while other stones which are singly refractive show only a single shadow or reading on the scale.

Generally speaking, gemstones which belong to the cubic system are singly refractive while all other crystal systems are of the double refraction type.

Singly refractive stones are diamonds, fluorspar and garnets.

Immersion methods

As indicated in the previous chapter, the use of the refractometer in testing the refractive index of stones is of value when testing stones with flat surfaces. It cannot, however, be used when investigating stones which are rough or have been carved. It is very often necessary for the rockhound to test rough material gathered on field trips and another method has been devised to give a test, if not accurate to the degree that a refractometer is accurate, at least sufficiently accurate to enable the individual to obtain a fairly good idea of the refractive index.

This method is known as the 'immersion method' and consists of placing the stone in a liquid with a known refractive index and then observing the result. If, for example, the stone and the liquid have identical refractive indices, then the outline of the stone will disappear or will become merged with the liquid. This can be best explained by placing a clear lump of ice in a tumbler of water. When this is observed from the side there is little or no outline visible which means, as we already appreciate, that the refractive indices of the two substances are almost identical.

The only equipment required for this test is a small glass beaker or dish and a selection of liquids which are readily obtainable and which have known refractive indices. There is a considerable range of liquids with refractive indices which are suitable for gem testing purposes and a few of these are listed below:

LIQUID	REFRACTIVE INDEX
Carbon tetrachloride	1·46
Toluene	1·50
Ethylene dibromide	1·54
Bromoform	1·59
Methylene iodide	1·75

Care must be taken when carrying out these tests to ensure that before the stone is transferred from one liquid to another it is thoroughly cleaned and dried, otherwise the different liquids will become contaminated and the known refractive indices will be altered.

This method of testing is also extremely useful for checking cut stones which the owner suspects might be doublets or triplets, that is stones of various types such as diamond and quartz which have been cemented together and then cut in such a fashion that they resemble the diamond.

Birefringence

Birefringence, or double refraction as it is more commonly called, is an extraordinary and very interesting feature of certain gemstones and other transparent minerals. To a lesser or greater extent it occurs in all minerals which do not crystallize in the cubic system, and gemmologists have, for the want of better terms, classified the cubic system which has no birefringence as *isotropic* and all other systems which do exhibit birefringence as *anisotropic*.

The terms are derived from the Greek and aptly describe the cause of double refraction—*iso* means equal or similar, while *aniso* means unequal.

Therefore, these two terms when applied to light rays indicate that in the cubic system the light rays entering the stone are similar while the light rays which enter any other stone are travelling at different velocities and are therefore unequal. It is these rays of unequal velocities which cause the double refraction.

The most common example of double refraction is observed in clear calcite (Iceland Spar). If a clear piece of this material is placed on top of writing, two very distinct images can be seen. In most other minerals the double refraction is, however, so small that it can hardly be observed with the naked eye and, even with the use of a strong glass, the double refraction is barely discernible in stones such as beryl.

Crystals of the tetragonal system do not exhibit double refraction when viewed along the direction of the 'c' or vertical axis, while, in the orthorhombic, monoclinic and triclinic systems, there are two directions in which birefringence is not observed. It is very difficult, therefore, for the amateur to obtain much real value from this aspect of gem and mineral study. It is, however, interesting to note that glass, from which imitation gems are made, is isotropic and because the refractive index of glass is 1·50 to 1·67, a bracket into which no other isotropic mineral falls, it provides yet another factor to assist in determining whether a stone is paste or genuine.

Hardness

All minerals have a definite hardness which ranges from the softest known mineral—talc, to the hardest—diamond.

For simplicity, the various hardnesses of all minerals have been listed under what is known as Mohs' scale. This scale is accepted internationally and grades the various hardnesses of minerals from 1 to 10. A rough guide is shown below:

1	Talc
2	Gypsum
3	Calcite
4	Apatite, fluorspar
5	Dioptase
6	Epidote, nephrite
7	Quartz
8	Topaz
9	Corundum
10	Diamond

This scale shows only the ascending order of hardness, but does not indicate the relative hardness of one material as compared with another. If we wanted to know the relative hardness, we would have to refer to the far more complicated and little known scale introduced by Rosiwal which shows the actual difference in hardness between minerals. A few examples are listed below:

1/33	Talc
1/4	Gypsum
4·5	Calcite
5	Fluorspar
6·5	Apatite
120	Quartz
175	Topaz
1 000	Corundum
140 000	Diamond

As can be seen, the tremendous difference in the various hardnesses as illustrated by the Rosiwal scale, makes the determination of hardness very much more difficult than the simple Mohs' scale. For this reason, Mohs' scale has now been accepted on an international basis and it shows, with sufficient clarity, the various steps in the ladder.

Checking the hardness of a piece of material is a relatively simple process if one has a good set of 'hardness pencils', but if these are not available, one can use stones or other instruments of known hardness to test the scratchability of the material. A simple guide is:

1　if a material can be scratched by a finger-nail, it will have a hardness of less than 2·5
2　if it can be scratched by a knife blade, it will be less than 5·5
3　if it can scratch glass, it must be harder than 5·5
4　if it can be scratched by a good file, it must be less than 6·5
5　if it can scratch a piece of quartz, it must be harder than 7.

These are simple basic rules and should be used with care because some stones, such as emerald, although fairly hard are nevertheless brittle and they could easily be damaged by a knife blade or file. It must also be remembered that a crystal which has scratches on its face will drop in value and it is recommended that wherever possible, the material being tested should be used to scratch stones of known hardness which have been retained for this purpose. Always start with material which you know is softer and work upwards.

Specific gravity

There are several recognized methods of testing the specific gravity of stones. The two most acceptable methods in use in the gemstone trade are the hydrostatic and the heavy liquid method. It is therefore intended to cover only these methods in this book.

Hydrostatic method

Specific gravity can be defined as the 'mass of a body compared with the mass of an equal volume of pure water at 4° Celsius'.

For this method of testing it is necessary to obtain a simple but nevertheless accurate chemical balance and an accurate set of jewellers' weights.

The first stage is to weigh the stone in air, note the reading and then weigh the stone in water. The apparent loss in mass is the mass of the water which has been displaced by the stone.

An example of this is:

Mass of stone in air	12·00 cts
Mass of stone in water	9·3 cts
Loss of mass in water	2·7 cts

$$\text{Specific gravity} = \frac{\text{mass in air}}{\text{loss in mass}} = \frac{12 \cdot 00}{2 \cdot 7} = 4 \cdot 46$$

A quick reference to our tables shows that zircon is one of the very few stones with a specific gravity in that range, so the field has been narrowed down still further.

Heavy liquid method

This method is only a very rough guide and should only be used for field tests and not as a final proof.

The liquids commonly used for testing are:

Bromoform—specific gravity 2·9
Methylene iodide—specific gravity 3·33
Clerici solution—specific gravity 4·15.

In order to increase the range of these liquids they can be diluted with benzine or alcohol. Thus, the rockhound who wishes to conduct field tests could have several different bottles containing liquids of various known specific gravities.

Care must be taken when carrying out tests on mineral specimens to ensure that the stone is clean and dry and, if the stone is transferred from one bottle to another, care must once again be taken to ensure that all liquid is dried off the stone and the tongs before the transfer is made. Failure to do this will upset the known specific gravities of the various bottles by contaminating them with liquid of a different specific gravity.

To dilute any of the liquids, one must decide beforehand the new specific gravity which is required. A good guide, however, is to select a number of fairly common gemstones such as:

Quartz—specific gravity 2·65

Emerald—specific gravity 2·71

Tourmaline—specific gravity 3·05

Topaz (white)—specific gravity 3·56

Pyrope—specific gravity 3·75

Corundum—specific gravity 3·99.

Take the liquid with a specific gravity higher than the stone in question and place a small quantity in a bottle. Then place a small piece of the stone (preferably cut and polished) in the liquid. The stone which is known as the 'indicator' will float on the liquid. Then, with a dropper, add the alcohol drop by drop, stirring the mixture continuously with a glass rod. When the indicator begins to sink and remains suspended in the mixture or only rises very slowly, the correct specific gravity has been achieved. The same method may now be used to dilute the other liquids using indicators of various known specific gravities until the full range required has been obtained.

To test specimens obtained in the field a small clean portion is placed in the various mixtures until it either remains suspended in one liquid or sinks in one and remains floating in the bottle with the next higher specific gravity. The true specific gravity or the limited range between two known specific gravities is thus established and the range is narrowed still further.

Under no circumstances should porous material such as opal, turquoise or chrysocolla be subjected to heavy liquid tests because the stone could be ruined by absorbing the liquid.

Actual testing sequence

On the previous pages the various elementary tests have been set out which will enable the rockhound to determine with a fair amount of accuracy, the material or stone being tested.

Each step in the ladder is important and must be faithfully followed if the desired result is to be obtained. It is strongly recommended that the following sequence is adhered to:

1 Study the crystal and ascertain to which crystal system the material belongs.
2 Note the colour of the material with the help of the list on page 23. The information gathered from the first two steps will limit the number of stones to be studied.
3 If a refractometer is available, check the refractive index.
4 Check the hardness of the stone, ensuring that as little damage as possible is done to the material being tested.
5 Then, if there is still doubt, check the specific gravity and the final set of facts should provide the answer.

For example, if we find:

1 the crystal system is hexagonal,
2 the stone is blue,
3 the refractive index is $1·76$,
4 the hardness is $9·0$,
5 the specific gravity is $3·99$,

it is almost certain that the material will be corundum (sapphire).

Streak test

The streak test is sometimes used when testing the softer range of minerals, but is seldom of any particular value when testing gemstones. True gemstones are usually harder than the streak plate and, if a streak can be left, it is more often than not white. It is nevertheless used fairly frequently in the field to narrow down the group of possible minerals to which the specimen belongs.

The only equipment required for this test is a small unglazed porcelain tile. The material being tested is drawn sharply across the tile surface and the colour of the streak noted.

The test undoubtedly has certain advantages and to assist those who wish to use it a selection of the more common minerals and the colour of the streak is appended below:

Agate—white
Alexandrite—white
Almandine garnet—white
Amazonite—white
Amethyst—white
Apatite—white to yellowish-grey
Aquamarine—white

Aventurine—white
Azurite—bright blue
Brucite—white
Carnelian—white
Cassiterite—white to pale yellow
Chalcedony—white
Chiastolite—white to pale grey
Chrysoberyl—white
Chrysocolla—pale green
Chrysoprase—white
Citrine—white
Cordierite—white
Epidote—grey
Fluorspar—white
Haematite—brown to red
Jade—white
Jasper—white
Kyanite—white
Labradorite—white
Malachite—light green
Scapolite—white
Sodalite—white
Spinel—white
Spodumene—white
Staurolite—brownish-white
Thulite—white to pale pink
Topaz—white
Tourmaline—white
Zircon—white

Identification tables in colour groups

NAME	MINERAL GROUP	HARD-NESS	SPECIFIC GRAVITY	REFRACTIVE INDEX	*
Green					
Alexandrite	chrysoberyl	8·5	3·65	1·74-1·75	tp-tl
Amazonite	feldspar	6-6·5	2·54-2·69	—	o
Apatite	apatite	5	3·17-3·23	1·64-1·65	tp
Aventurine quartz	quartz	7	2·65	1·54-1·55	tl-o
Bowenite	serpentine	3-4	2·5-2·7	1·49-1·57	tl-o
Chalcedony (mtorolite)	quartz	7	2·52-2·8	—	o
Cymophane (cat's eye)	chrysoberyl	8·5	3·65	1·74-1·75	tp-tl
Chrysocolla	copper	2-4	2-2·54	—	o
Chrysoprase	quartz	7	2·58-2·65	—	o
Demantoid	garnet	6·5-7	3·83-3·96	1·89	tp
Diopside	pyroxene	5·5	3·25-3·4	1·64-1·70	tp-tl
Emerald	beryl	7·5	2·64-2·73	1·58-1·59	tp
Epidote	epidote	7	3·25-3·5	1·72-1·78	tp-o
Fluorite	fluorspar	4	3·01-3·25	1·43	tp
Heliodor (yellow-green)	beryl	7·5	2·72-2·73	1·57-1·58	tp
Heliotrope (bloodstone)	quartz	7	2·5-2·8	—	o
Hiddenite	spodumene	6·5-7	3·2	1·6-1·67	tp
Jade (nephrite)	amphibole	5-6	2·9-3·1	—	o
Malachite	copper	3·5-4	3·8-4·1	—	o
Serpentine	serpentine	3-4	2·5-2·7	—	o
Soapstone	talc	1-2	2·7-2·8	—	o
Tourmaline	tourmaline	7-7·5	3·06-3·12	1·62-1·65	tp
Red—pink					
Almandine	garnet	7·5-8	3·83-4·20	1·80	tp
Carnelian	quartz	7	2·5-2·8	—	tl-o
Fluorite	fluorspar	4	3·01-3·25	1·43	tp
Jasper	quartz	7	2·5-2·8	—	o
Kunzite	spodumene	6·5-7	3·2	1·66-1·67	tp

Morganite	beryl	7·5	2·8–2·87	1·58–1·59	tp
Pyrope	garnet	7–7·5	3·65–3·80	1·74	tp
Rose quartz	quartz	7	2·6–2·7	1·54–1·55	tp
Rubelite	tourmaline	7–7·5	3·09–3·15	1·62–1·65	tp
Ruby	corundum	9	3·9–4·14	1·76–1·77	tp
Spinel	spinel	8	3·5–4·1	1·72	tp-o
Sunstone	feldspar	6–6·5	2·66	1·52–1·53	tp-tl
Thulite	zoisite	6–6·5	3·4–3·48	—	o

Blue—violet

Almandine	garnet	7·5–8	3·83–4·20	1·80	tp-tl
Apatite	apatite	5	3·15–3·23	1·64–1·65	tp
Amethyst	quartz	7	2·6–2·7	1·54–1·55	tp-tl
Aquamarine	beryl	7–7·5	2·67–2·71	1·57–1·58	tp
Azurite	copper	3·5–4	3·8–3·83	—	o
Chrysocolla	copper	2–4	2·0–2·42	—	o
Corderite (iolite)	corderite	7–7·5	2·57–2·66	1·54–1·55	tp
Dumortierite	dumortierite	7	3·24–3·28	—	o
Euclase	beryl	7·5–8	3·1–3·13	1·64–1·67	tp-o
Fluorite	fluorspar	4	3·01–3·25	1·43	tp
Indicolite	tourmaline	7·5	3·1–3·12	1·62–1·64	tp
Kyanite	kyanite	4–7	3·56–3·67	1·71–1·73	tp-o
Sapphire	corundum	9	4·01–4·09	1·76–1·77	tp
Sodalite	sodalite	5–6	2·2–2·4	—	o
Topaz	topaz	8	3·5–3·52	1·60–1·62	tp

Brown—yellow

Carnelian	quartz	7	2·5–2·8	—	o
Chiastolite	andalucite	7·5	3·22–3·29	—	o
Cymophane (cat's eye)	chrysoberyl	8·5	3·65	1·74–1·75	tp
Citrine	quartz	7	2·65–2·7	1·54–1·55	tp
Dravite	tourmaline	7·25	3·09–3·15	1·61–1·63	tp-tl
Epidote	epidote	7	3·25–3·5	1·75–1·81	tp
Golden beryl	beryl	7·5	2·64–2·73	1·58–1·59	tp
Hessonite	garnet	6	3·50–3·70	1·74	tp
Phenakite	phenakite	7·5–8	3·0	1·65–1·67	tp-tl
Smoky quartz	quartz	7	2·65–2·66	1·54–1·55	tp-tl
Tiger's eye	quartz	7	2·65	—	o
Zircon	zircon	7·5–8	4·0–4·65	1·92–1·98	tp

Agate (many different colours, banded and dendritic)	quartz	7	2·5–2·8	—	o
Brucite (white)	brucite	2·5	2·4	—	o
Chalcedony (white)	quartz	7	2·5–2·8	—	o
Diamond (usually colourless)	diamond	10	3·32–3·54	2·41	tp–o
Goshenite (colourless)	beryl	7·5	2·67–2·71	1·58–1·59	tp
Haematite (metallic black)	iron	6·5	4·9–5·3	—	o
Labradorite (colourless with schiller of greens and blue)	feldspar	6	2·62–2·76	1·56–1·57	tl
Marble (various blobs and streaks)	limestone	3–3·5	2·65–2·85	—	o
Milky quartz (white with pale blue shades)	quartz	7	2·6–2·7	1·54–1·55	tl
Moonstone (colourless with schiller of blue or silver)	feldspar	6	2·62–2·67	1·56–1·57	tl
Obsidian (black to dark green)	glassy lava	5–5·5	2·5–2·6	1·5	tl
Onyx (black and white bands)	quartz	7	2·5–2·8	—	o
Oppalite (various colours)	quartz	5–6	2·0	—	o
Rock crystal (colourless)	quartz	7	2·64–2·66	1·54–1·55	tp
Sardonyx (red or brown and white bands)	quartz	7	2·64–2·66	—	o
Scapolite (colourless)	scapolite	5–6	2·54–2·77	1·55–1·57	tp–o
Schorl (black)	tourmaline	7	3·09–3·15	—	o
Sphene (colourless to red)	sphene	5·5	3·53	1·90–2·03	o

Staurolite staurolite (reddish-brown to black)	7–7·5	3·65–3·78	—	o
Topaz topaz (colourless)	8	3·56–3·6	1·62–1·63	tp
Wood opal quartz (various colours chiefly reds and greens)	7	2·0	—	o
Unakite epidote/feldspar (red, brown and yellow-green)	6	2·8–3·1	—	o
Zircon zircon (colourless)	7·5	4·0–4·65	1·93–1·99	tp

Gemstones and Crystals
found in Rhodesia

Although the main object behind this book is gemstones of Rhodesia, it could never be complete without a reference to some of the better formed crystals and interesting minerals which do not produce gem material, but are always welcome in a collection of specimens. It is therefore intended to devote this section to everything which the collector or gemmologist may find of interest in Rhodesia.

True gemstones are obtained from some twenty different mineral groups which in turn can be broken down into any number of sub-groups. In order to simplify the following text, stones will be listed alphabetically under each mineral group. Thus agate will appear under quartz and emerald under beryl.

It was as far back as 1903 that prospectors first became aware of the existence of gemstones in Rhodesia. The first discovery was made by a Mr H. R. Moir at the site where the old road from Tuli to Gwelo crossed the Somabula Spruit. Mr Moir who had had considerable experience on the Vaal alluvial diamond diggings immediately recognized the diamond potential of the gravels in the vicinity of the stream and obtained certain rights to mine.

During the years that followed, the Somabula fields were worked spasmodically by various companies and individuals who, in addition to finding diamonds, located small quantities of sapphire, ruby, chrysoberyl and topaz.

The Somabula fields were the first real indication that gemstone deposits existed in Rhodesia. It was not, however, until 1956, fifty-three years after the initial find, that the discovery of emeralds at Sandawana sparked off the gemstone fever which has gripped the country ever since.

The search for gemstones is no longer confined to emeralds and diamonds, but covers a vast field from agates to wood opal and specimens of the various industrial minerals, which may not even have gemstone potential, but are of interest because of their colour or crystal structure.

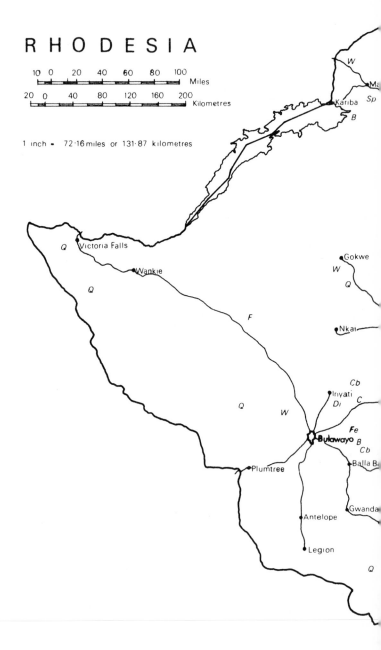

R H O D E S I A

10 0   20   40   60   80   100
Miles

20 0   40   80   120 160 200
Kilometres

1 inch = 72·16 miles or 131·87 kilometres

W

Ma

Sp

Kariba

B

Q Victoria Falls

Gokwe

W

Q

Wankie

Nkai

F

Cb

Inyati   C

Di

Q   W

Fe

Bulawayo B

Cb

Balla B

Plumtree

Gwanda

Antelope

Legion

Q

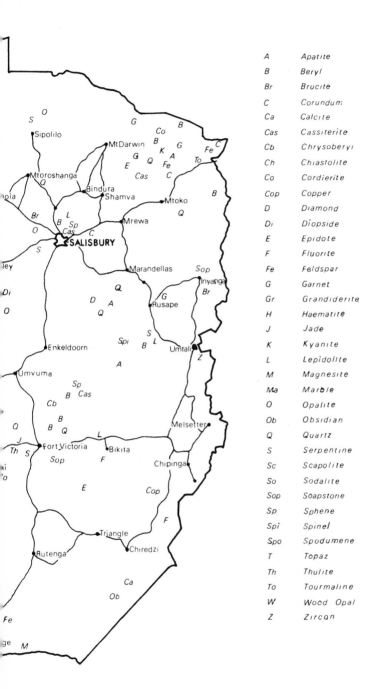

A	Apatite
B	Beryl
Br	Brucite
C	Corundum
Ca	Calcite
Cas	Cassiterite
Cb	Chrysoberyl
Ch	Chiastolite
Co	Cordierite
Cop	Copper
D	Diamond
Di	Diopside
E	Epidote
F	Fluorite
Fe	Feldspar
G	Garnet
Gr	Grandiderite
H	Haematite
J	Jade
K	Kyanite
L	Lepidolite
M	Magnesite
Ma	Marble
O	Opalite
Ob	Obsidian
Q	Quartz
S	Serpentine
Sc	Scapolite
So	Sodalite
Sop	Soapstone
Sp	Sphene
Spi	Spinel
Spo	Spodumene
T	Topaz
Th	Thulite
To	Tourmaline
W	Wood Opal
Z	Zircon

All the old beryl mines have been re-pegged and a certain quantity of aquamarine, heliodor and golden beryl recovered, but the best gemstone mines which have been discovered in Rhodesia, apart from the emerald mines, are situated in areas which were not worked for commercial beryl in the first instance. Examples of these mines are the St Anne's at Miami and the Novello in Fort Victoria. Doubtless there are others and more will be found, but these two pegmatite properties have been worked continuously for many years and show no signs of being worked out.

It is interesting to note that these two properties have certain unique features which make them different to the other gemstone properties in the country.

St Anne's mine has produced possibly half the aquamarine, heliodor, golden beryl and goshenite which has been mined in Rhodesia. In addition to this, however, St Anne's is the only Rhodesian mine which has ever produced gem quality blue topaz. It has also produced half Rhodesia's output of gem tourmaline and a considerable quantity of specimens and garnets—not a bad record for any mine.

The Novello mine, like the St Anne's, can also claim to be the only producer of a certain gemstone—alexandrite. No other property in the country can claim this honour and although a lot of the alexandrite is not of true gem quality, some of the world's finest specimens have been produced from this property. It is also possible that the Novello is the only mine in the world today which is producing alexandrite of a reasonable quality.

Another interesting factor which led to the discovery of gemstones in Rhodesia and the establishment of the local industry, goes back to the early production of commercial beryl in the 1950s. In those days the miners were interested only in mining commercial beryl and the fact that some of it might have been blue or gold made no difference. Astute buyers in America were, however, more discerning when it came to sorting the commercial beryl, and a considerable quantity of good quality aquamarine eventually found its way to Idar-Oberstein in Germany. Idar-Oberstein has long been considered the centre of the world's gem cutting industry and the sight of this new aquamarine from Rhodesia has brought many top quality cutters and dealers to our country. It is to these people that a lot of our thanks must go for helping to put Rhodesia on the gemstone map of the world.

APATITE (Fig. 1, page 33)
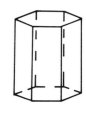
Hardness: 4-5
Specific gravity: 3·15-3·23
Refractive index: 1·63-1·65
Crystal system: hexagonal or massive
Colour: from almost colourless through yellow to green and blue

Apatite, although not a true gemstone because it lacks the hardness required to withstand scratching, is nevertheless a fairly popular stone for small carvings and brooches. It is also a fairly popular collector's piece, particularly the bigger crystals which often occur in the pegmatites. Some cut stones have also been known to exhibit fairly strong chatoyancy.

This mineral is also an important source of phosphate and as such is widely used in the manufacture of fertilizers. The most important occurrences of the industrial mineral in this country are located on carbonate rich plugs (ring complexes) of Dorowa and Shawa some sixty kilometres south-east of Rusape in the Buhera Tribal Trust Land. Crystalline material has also been recovered from the Marandellas and Fungwe areas.

BERYL
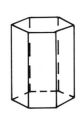
Hardness: 7·5-8
Specific gravity: 2·67-2·71
Refractive index: 1·57-1·60
Crystal system: hexagonal
Colour: Aquamarine—blue
Emerald—green
Golden beryl—deep yellow to golden brown
Heliodor—yellow to greenish-yellow
Morganite—pale rose to rose-pink
Goshenite—colourless

The beryl group undoubtedly forms the most valuable gemstone group in Rhodesia. It is also one of the stones favoured by the collector of specimens because so many perfect and near-perfect crystals are found in sizes ranging from a few millimetres in height to a metre or more. The larger size crystals are seldom gem quality, although they may contain pools of gemmy material, but unless the pools are of first class quality, it is better to retain the crystal intact as a specimen.

Beryl is always associated with the pegmatites and is fairly common throughout the northern part of Rhodesia. It also occurs in the Filabusi, Belingwe, Fort Victoria and Sabi/Odzi areas.

Emerald (Fig. 3, page 34)

The emerald is possibly the most valuable gemstone in the world today. Clean stones of a good colour are undoubtedly highly prized and much sought after. Rhodesia is extremely lucky in this respect, because the Sandawana stones have the finest colour known in emeralds and are prized in all the gemstone markets the world over.

Emerald was first discovered in the Belingwe District in 1956. The discoverers, two well known Rhodesian prospectors, Bob Contat and Corrie Oosthuizen, followed up the indications in riverbeds to what is now known as the Sandawana mine. It was in fact these two who gave the deposit the name of Sandawana and they, together with the original agent, Dan E. Mayers, first put this fabulous stone on the market.

Prospecting for emeralds soon became a major pastime in Rhodesia and gradually new deposits were located, several small ones in the Belingwe area, others near Filabusi, Fort Victoria, Felixburg and Odzi. As the search for emeralds widens, new deposits are likely to be discovered and it is possible that some of these may even equal the Sandawana one.

Aquamarine, heliodor, golden beryl, morganite and goshenite (Fig. 4, page 35)

Good quality aquamarine and golden beryl have been discovered in the Miami, Urungwe, Fungwe and Mtoko areas and some beautiful stones have been cut from this material. Heliodor, morganite and goshenite have also been produced from these areas, but the quality and quantity is not up to the standard required for first class jewellery. Recently an unusual black beryl was discovered in the Filabusi area, but this material has little or no value outside the specimen market. Gem quality beryl has

Fig. 1   Apatite

Fig. 2   Calcite

Fig. 3 Emerald

Fig. 4 Aquamarine and golden beryl

Fig. 5 Travertine marble

Fig. 6 Alexandrite

Fig. 7   Chiastolite

Fig. 8 Malachite

Fig. 9 Cordierite

Fig. 10   Sapphire, ruby, corundum

Fig. 11 Diamonds

also been discovered in the emerald areas, but with the main activity directed towards emerald, little or nothing is done on the semi-precious materials.

BRUCITE

Hardness: 2·5
Specific gravity: 2·4
Refractive index: opaque
Crystal structure: massive, sometimes found in small hexagonal crystals
Colour: white

A source of magnesium ore and not a true gemstone. It is, however, a very interesting specimen material and can be carved with a fair amount of success. The stone also has a perfect cleavage and frequently cleaves into thin, curved sheets.

Brucite is fairly common and has been located in the Inyanga and Gatooma districts and can generally be found throughout the length and breadth of the Great Dyke.

CALCITE (ICELAND SPAR)

Hardness: 3-3·5
Specific gravity: 2·6-2·8
Refractive index: 1·66
Crystal system: hexagonal
Colour: colourless or pastel shades of yellow, pink, blue and green

Calcite (Fig. 2, page 32)

Calcite is not a recognized gemstone, but in its clear and translucent form can be used for carvings and cabochons which make rather pleasing specimens.

The stone is widely distributed throughout Rhodesia, but only a very small quantity is of value to the collector. The better material is located in the Victoria district and to a limited extent in Urungwe. Clear specimens have a very marked double refraction (double image) which gives them an additional value in the optical instrument trade.

Calcite has a perfect cleavage parallel to the rhombohedral faces as depicted in the sketch on page 42.

Well formed calcite crystals can frequently be located in cavities underlying limestone deposits and in limestone caves. The stalactites and stalagmites which are formed by the action of water seeping through the limestone and dissolving certain solids are almost pure calcite.

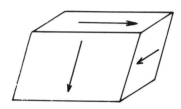

Travertine (Fig. 5, page 36)

Springs in limestone areas dissolve the calcite and deposit it on the surface to form travertine, a brown form of banded opaque calcite which is a fairly popular carving material and which takes a fairly good polish. Unfortunately, it only has a hardness of 3 and is therefore not often used as a gemstone.

Tufa

Like travertine, tufa is also dissolved calcite deposited by springs and streams. It is usually spongy or porous and therefore of value only as a specimen.

CASSITERITE

Hardness: 6–7
Specific gravity: 6·8–7·1
Refractive index: opaque
Crystal structure: massive, granular or tetragonal
Colour: brown to brownish-black

Cassiterite is actually tinstone and the most important source of tin. It is not a true gemstone, although it can be cut and polished. The main interest from the rockhound's point of view is the crystal formation which is very distinctive and well formed and can be found in a great variety of shapes and sizes.

Good quality material is found in the pegmatites around Kamativi, Bikita, Urungwe, Mtoko and in the vicinity of Salisbury.

CHRYSOBERYL

Hardness: 8·5
Specific gravity: 3·5-3·84
Refractive index: 1·74-1·75
Crystal system: orthorhombic
Colour: alexandrite-green (daylight)
cymophane: honey
through yellow to
pale green

Alexandrite (Fig. 6, page 36)

There are two distinct types of chrysoberyl used in the gemstone industry, alexandrite and cymophane. Alexandrite is a
unique stone which exhibits an emerald green colour in daylight
and a deep red under artificial light. Chromium is responsible
for the colouring of this stone and the variation under different
types of light is due to differential absorption of daylight and
artificial light. The stones show a very marked pleochroism from
dark green to blue green and violet to rose red.

Alexandrite is extremely rare today and very little true gem
material is being mined anywhere in the world. Rhodesia's deposit
on the Novello claims in the Victoria district is possibly the only
producer of any consequence.

Cymophane (cat's eye)

Better known as chrysoberyl, cat's eye is much more common
than alexandrite and has been discovered in the Victoria, Filabusi
and Karoi/Miami areas. The best quality gemstone material is,
however, found in Karoi and some excellent cat's eyes have been
cut from the stones mined there.

Chrysoberyl is always associated with pegmatites when found
in situ, but possibly the best hunting ground is in the alluvial
deposits which flank the hard pegmatites—material recovered
from here is usually fairly clean and more easily examined.

The cat's eye effect or chatoyancy in these stones is caused by
lines of minute crystalline rods or fibres which give the remark-
able and beautiful effect of colour movement in the stone when
it has been cut *en cabochon*.

CHIASTOLITE (andalusite) (Fig. 7, page 37)

Hardness: 7·5
Specific gravity: 3·22–3·29
Refractive index: 1·46
Crystal system: orthorhombic
Colour: brownish-red to light
    grey

Chiastolite, an altered form of andalusite is not a common form of gemstone, but is a very popular specimen collector's piece. The material readily forms chunky crystals which have very distinct dark inclusions which are arranged in the form of a cross as indicated above.

Gemmy material in both chiastolite and andalusite has been located, chiefly in Spain, and it is possible that this country may yet produce some of worthwhile cutting quality. The best material seen from Rhodesia has been mined in the Miami/Urungwe areas but it is possible that more sources of this material will be located in the southern parts of the country.

COPPER

Copper is one of the most versatile minerals known to man. In its metallic form, it serves as a conductor of heat or electricity, and is used in the manufacture of many varied items such as water-piping, cooking utensils and ornaments. In its mineral form it gives us a wide variety of gemstones and specimens which are enthusiastically sought after. Because of the wide range in colour, hardness and crystal formation between the various forms of gemstones, it is necessary to treat each stone separately.

Azurite

Hardness: 3·5–4
Specific gravity: 3·8–3·83
Refractive index: usually opaque
Crystal system: monoclinic,
botryoidal or massive
Colour: blue (various shades)

Azurite is a most attractive stone, producing good cabochon, carving and specimen material. It occurs in zones of weathering in copper deposits, often in association with malachite.

44

It can be located in small quantites in the Sinoia and Devuli Ranch areas.

Chrysocolla
Hardness: 2·5-4
Specific gravity: 2·0-2·42
Refractive index: opaque
Crystal system: amorphous, massive and botryoidal
Colour: pale green to pale blue

Chrysocolla is a most acceptable gemstone, often resembling turquoise and sometimes sold as such. It is also a popular collector's piece. It is often associated with malachite and azurite and has been discovered in small quantities on the Elephant mine, Devuli ranch.

Dioptase
Hardness: 5
Specific gravity: 3·27-3·35
Refractive index: 1·64-1·70
Crystal system: hexagonal
Colour: emerald green

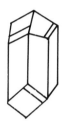

Dioptase is located in small quantities between the Alaska and Copper Queen mines in the Sinoia district. The crystals are seldom large enough to cut and polish, but some that have been cut are equal to the best emerald in colour and life. Because of its very close resemblance to emerald, the stone has been nicknamed 'copper-emerald'.

Malachite (Fig. 8, page 38)
Hardness: 3·5-4
Specific gravity: 3·54-4·1
Refractive index: usually opaque
Crystal system: monoclinic, massive or botryoidal
Colour: green (shades) with black spots or concentric bands

This is the most popular copper gemstone used extensively in jewellery and the carving trade and is also an important collector's piece. It is associated with azurite and copper pyrites in zones of copper oxidation. It is not very common in Rhodesia, but has been located in the Sinoia district. The best quality material is obtained from the mineral-rich Katanga province of the Congo and is in worldwide demand.

CORDIERITE (Fig. 9, page 38)
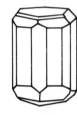
    Hardness: 7·5
    Specific gravity: 2·57–2·66
    Refractive index: 1·55
    Crystal system: orthorhombic or
        massive, often scaly or granular
    Colour: blue (shades)

Cordierite, also known as iolite or 'water sapphire', is a silicate of aluminium, iron and magnesium. Good specimens have a very pleasing blue colour showing very marked pleochroism from blue to grey when turned through a right angle. Good gem quality material is not common but various deposits in Rhodesia, chiefly in the Urungwe and Mtoko areas, have produced some first class gemstones. Other sources are located in the Victoria district.

Because of the scarcity of good gem material, there is a constant demand for specimen and cutting quality stones. The greatest demand comes, however, from the rockhound and collector, because although the stone might have a good sapphire blue colour, it lacks the brilliance and sparkle of the true sapphire and is more popular in display cases because of its rarity.

CORUNDUM (Fig. 10, page 39)
    Hardness: 9
    Specific gravity: 3·99–4·00
    Refractive index: 1·76–1·77
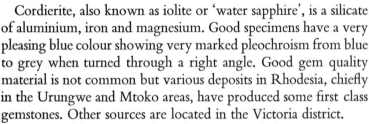
    Crystal system: hexagonal, usually columnar or barrel-shaped
    Colour: red—ruby
          blue—sapphire
          orange—padparadscha
          Other colours particularly in pastel shades known in the trade as 'fancy sapphires'
Ruby and sapphire are second only to the diamond in hardness

and together with diamond and emerald form what is known as the true precious stones group. The value of precious stones far exceeds the value of any other gemstone with the possible exception of alexandrite. Colouring in ruby is due to chromic oxide and in sapphire to the presence of titanium and iron.

The corundum group is mined chiefly in the East: ruby from Ceylon, Burma and Siam, and sapphire from Burma, Kashmir and Ceylon. Other sources of these stones are East Africa, Australia, Malawi and U.S.A.

Recently discoveries of sapphire and ruby material have been made in Rhodesia, from both the Mtoko and Goromonzi districts. Several stones have been cut from the sapphire and show a pleasing light blue to Kashmir blue colour while another deposit near Goromonzi has produced some very interesting dark star sapphires but at the time of writing, the ruby material has not been fully tested, although it shows considerable possibilities for good clean small stones.

These new ruby crystals will be of interest as specimens if nothing else because each crystal is fully encased in a pale green translucent skin of talc/serpentine-like material.

Sapphires and rubies were first discovered in Rhodesia in the Somabula gravels during 1903. These stones were rather small in size and only a limited number were cuttable. Near ruby corundum has also been discovered in the Beit Bridge area but insufficient work has been done to either prove or disprove the possibility of a good deposit.

DIAMOND (Fig. 11, page 40)

Hardness: 10
Specific gravity: 3·32–3·54
Refractive index: 2·42
Crystal system: cubic
Colour: usually colourless, but also has a wide variety of colours including yellow, brown, blue, red and pink

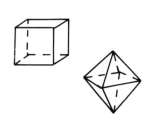

The diamond is the hardest substance known to man and was possibly the first gemstone to attract interest. It was known in the Far East, particularly India, long before the birth of Christ. For centuries India was the only producer of quality diamonds. Then, in the early 1700s, diamonds were discovered in Brazil and that country became the most important producer of gem quality stones, a position which it retained until diamonds were discovered in South Africa on the Vaal and Orange rivers in 1860 and at Kimberley in the 1870s. These South African diamonds were the first to be found in their true host rock. Volcanic crater pipes containing a rock known as blue ground or kimberlite, named after Kimberley where the first pipe was discovered is the true host. The Kimberley pipe was worked for many years, firstly by single claim holders and finally by De Beer's and now constitutes what South Africans fondly refer to as the 'Big Hole'.

Following the South African discovery, deposits were found in the Congo, Tanzania, Siberia, South West Africa and, last but not least, Rhodesia. No country can, however, challenge South Africa and South West Africa's position as the principal gem diamond producers of the world. These two countries are currently producing something in excess of 50 per cent of the total world gem requirements. South Africa, in addition to producing the greatest quantity of diamonds, is also responsible for producing some of the biggest diamonds known. First and foremost in this field is the Cullinan diamond which was discovered at the Premier mine near Pretoria in 1905. The uncut stone weighed 3 106 carats and was finally cut into nine major stones, the biggest of which is known as the Star of Africa or Cullinan and weighs 615 carats, and ninety-six lesser stones.

People are apt to think of the diamond only in its role as a jewel, but it is interesting to note that approximately eighty per cent of all the diamonds mined and one hundred per cent of all synthetic diamonds are used for purely industrial purposes. These diamonds are used in the form of dust to cut other gems, as chips or whole crystals to cut hard metals and ceramics and in diamond crowns for drilling through hard rock.

Over the years, diamonds have always been the most popular gemstone and although emerald or ruby may displace them from the top of the ladder every now and again, they persistently return to first place. The diamond is the only gemstone which consists of a single element—carbon in its pure crystalline form.

Diamonds were first discovered in Rhodesia at the Somabula fields by a Mr H. R. Moir. These stones were found in association with small rubies, sapphires and chrysoberyls in the rubble bed of an old river system which was extensively worked for several years following the initial discovery. Since that time the area has been investigated spasmodically by smallworkers and prospectors with varying degrees of success.

The Somabula diamond differs from most other known diamonds in that it has a greenish tinge in the rough. On cutting, however, the green disappears and usually leaves a remarkably clear and clean white stone. Experts are of the opinion that the green colouring is due almost entirely to a thin skin caused by radiation.

Kimberlite pipes are the accepted original host rock from which all diamonds have been derived and although Rhodesia can boast half a dozen such pipes, they all appear to be too young to have produced the Somabula stones. Search for new pipes and more careful examination of the known ones nevertheless continues and it is possible that the secret of Somabula will be discovered shortly.

Diamonds from alluvial beds have also been discovered in the Bulawayo, Gokwe, Beatrice, Featherstone and Darwin districts.

DIOPSIDE

Hardness: 5·5
Specific gravity: 3·25–3·4
Refractive index: 1·65–1·7
Crystal structure: monoclinic or
    massive
Colour: green

Diopside is not a true gemstone as it is too soft. It is seldom seen in the transparent form, but is nevertheless an interesting specimen even in the opaque form. Most material found in Rhodesia occurs as small grains in pyroxenite, norite and gabbro. It is, however, also associated with kimberlite pipes such as the Colossus pipe in the Bulawayo area. Chrome diopside is also associated with the serpentine bodies and may therefore occur along the Great Dyke.

DUMORTIERITE (Fig. 12, page 57)

Hardness: 7
Specific gravity: 3·24–3·28
Refractive index: 1·66–1·68
Crystal system: orthorhombic—usually massive

Colour: lavender to blue

Dumortierite has been located in the Lowveld near the Sabi River, and it has also been reported from the Urungwe area. Rhodesian material is frequently opaque and massive but has fairly good colour. Its most important use is in industry in the manufacture of ceramics and refractory materials, but because it is fairly hard, tough and durable and can take an excellent polish, it is always a welcome acquisition for the lapidary.

EPIDOTE (Fig. 13, page 58)

Hardness: 6-7
Specific gravity: 3·25-3·5
Refractive index: 1·73-1·76
Crystal system: monoclinic.
More than 200 forms known
Colour: tea coloured to yellowish-green

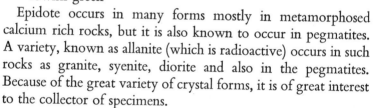

Epidote occurs in many forms mostly in metamorphosed calcium rich rocks, but it is also known to occur in pegmatites. A variety, known as allanite (which is radioactive) occurs in such rocks as granite, syenite, diorite and also in the pegmatites. Because of the great variety of crystal forms, it is of great interest to the collector of specimens.

A fairly high proportion of crystal material found in Rhodesia is of gemstone quality and can be cut into interesting ring and brooch stones. Clear stones show fairly strong pleochroism from tea colour to pale yellowish-green. The pleochroism is, however, most marked in the flat bladed crystals.

Most of the good material discovered to date comes from the Fungwe area, but it is possible that other deposits exist in the Urungwe and Victoria districts as well.

EUCLASE

Hardness: 7·5-8
Specific gravity: 3·1-3·13
Refractive index: 1·64-1·67
Crystal system: monoclinic, also massive
Colour: colourless, blue, yellow and green

Euclase, a beryllium orthosilicate could well have been included in the beryl group, but because it varies to such an extent from the normal aquamarine, etcetera, it is considered more correct to treat it as a separate mineral.

Euclase in its gem form is extremely rare in Rhodesia, although it is possible that the material does occur in drab yellow colourings in the massive form. Only a limited number of specimens of a deep blue colour have been seen to date and it is understood that these were discovered in the Mtoko area. It is, however, doubtful if any of this material has been cut in Rhodesia, but as with everything else some lucky rockhound may unknowingly have a very rare and valuable stone in his collection.

FELDSPAR

The feldspar group of minerals is fairly extensive. The best known are microcline, orthoclase and plagioclase.

Microcline is a potassium feldspar which crystallizes in the triclinic system while orthoclase, which has a similar chemical composition, crystallizes in the monoclinic system.

Plagioclase is the name given to describe the group of feldspars which vary in composition from albite sodium feldspar, to anorthite calcium feldspar. It is from this group that we obtain most of our feldspar gemstones which include such stones as amazonite, labradorite and sunstone.

Amazonite (Fig. 15, page 59)
Hardness: 6-6·5
Specific gravity: 2·54-2·69
Refractive index: opaque
Crystal system: triclinic
Colour: green or brick red with
white inclusions

Amazonite in green or blue-green is a fairly popular gemstone and it is also used extensively in the ornamental trade. The stone takes a good polish and is sufficiently hard to withstand scratching.

It is found in the Miami, Urungwe and Fungwe areas.

Labradorite and sunstone (Fig. 15, page 59)
Hardness: 6
Specific gravity: 2·62-2·76
Refractive index: 1·56-1·57

Crystal system: triclinic

Colour: labradorite—iridescent play of colours including green and blue

sunstone—milky colour with flashes of gold

Labradorite is a popular gemstone if the colours are strong and clear. Local material has not, however, reached this standard and the only recorded discoveries are from the Beitbridge area.

Sunstone, like labradorite, has to be well coloured to be popular. Some reasonable material has been located in the Beitbridge area, but considerably more work will have to be done before any worthwhile deposit is proved.

Unakite (Fig. 16, page 60)

A mixture of pink feldspar, green epidote and quartz which has been included in the feldspar group for the sake of simplicity.

Hardness: 6·5-7

Specific gravity: 2·65-2·70

Refractive index: opaque

Crystal system: usually massive

Colour: mottled pink and green

This is not a true gemstone, but has been used to good effect in brooches, bracelets and necklaces. It is also a popular carving material for such items as ash trays. It takes a fairly high polish and has become very popular in Europe and America.

Material of acceptable quality is fairly common throughout Rhodesia, but the best sources appear to be in the Bulawayo, Gwelo and Beitbridge areas.

FLUORSPAR (Fig. 14, page 58)

Hardness: 4

Specific gravity: 3·01-3·25

Refractive index: 1·43

Crystal system: cubic or massive

Colour: colourless when pure, also violet, blue, green, yellow and red

Fluorspar is not a recognized gemstone because it is too soft to retain a polish for long and because it is very difficult to cut. Those people who have tried find that the stone chips, fractures and peels when cutting, making it impossible to cut with any accuracy. It

cracks readily under very slight heat and should not therefore be cleaned in warm water.

The stone has a perfect cleavage and will readily cleave in four different directions parallel to the octahedral faces. One has only to establish the direction of one face to be able to cleave, with the use of a chisel, a perfect octahedron.

Because of its ability to cleave and difficulty experienced in faceting the material, together with the variety of colours often contained in one small specimen, it will always be a welcome addition to any collection.

Good quality material has been located in several areas in Rhodesia, but the best from the point of view of colour and clarity is the P & O mine deposit in the Victoria district and the Tinde deposit near Wankie.

Fluorspar is usually associated with pegmatites, but can be found elsewhere if the conditions are right. It is used as a flux in the steel industry and also in the manufacture of hydrofluoric acid which is commonly used for such purposes as neutralizing alkaline water.

GARNET (Fig. 17, page 61)

   Hardness: 6-8 (see table on page 54)
   Specific gravity: 3·5-4·20 (see
      table on page 54)
   Refractive index: 1·7 to 1·9 (see
      table on page 54)
   Crystal system: cubic and mas-
      sive
   Colour: blood red—pyrope
      purplish-red to brown-red—almandine
      green—demantoid, orange-brown—hessonite

Garnet is very widespread in Rhodesia but most of the material is not suitable for the gemstone industry. However, a considerable amount of the non-gemmy material can be found in a perfect crystal form and it is therefore a popular collector's item.

The most popular garnet is undoubtedly the pyrope, sometimes incorrectly called 'Cape ruby' because of its close resemblance to a ruby. This stone, when well cut and polished, makes a most attractive and brilliant gemstone. In value, however, it takes second place to the demantoid, which is extremely rare and is seldom found today.

Almandine and hessonite stones are fairly common in Rhodesia and although not as striking and beautiful as the first two, are nevertheless most welcome additions to any collection of gemstones or specimens.

Demantoid has only been discovered in one area in Rhodesia —the Chimanda Tribal Trust Land, near the Mazoe river, while pyrope has been mined in the Mtoko and Beitbridge areas. Almandine and hessonite have been found at Mtoko, Rusape/ Headlands, Urungwe, Chimanda, Beitbridge and several other localities.

Garnets usually occur in pegmatites but are also common in certain metamorphic rocks and kimberlites. As far as can be ascertained, no grossular (Transvaal jade) type of garnet has been discovered in Rhodesia.

Main types of garnet

Due to the great variety of garnets, it is not possible to show the true data in the standard table at the beginning of the section and, in order to clarify the position, a table showing the main varieties is given below:

NAME	HARDNESS	SPECIFIC GRAVITY	REFRACTIVE INDEX	COLOUR
Almandine	7·5–8	3·83–4·20	1·80	purplish-red
Andradite	6·5–7	3·80–3·90	1·89	brown
Demantoid	6·5–7	3·80–3·85	1·89	green
Grossular	7–7·5	3·60–3·70	1·75	green, pink or cream
Hessonite	6	3·50–3·70	1·74	orange
Pyrope	7–7·5	3·65–3·80	1·74	red

GRANDIDIERITE

Hardness: 7

Specific gravity: 3

Refractive index: 1·602–1·639

Crystal system: orthorhombic

Colour: blue

This is a complex boro-silicate mineral related to tourmaline, with all the attributes of a good quality gemstone. The stone is, however, extremely rare and the only specimens located to date in Rhodesia have been found in the pegmatites in the Miami area. The stones which have been brought in so far are generally too small and fractured to be of any value to the cutter. It is possible, however, that some bigger and better quality crystals will eventually be discovered and put on the market.

HAEMATITE (Fig. 18, page 61)

Hardness: from as low as 5·5 to nearly 7, gem material usually about 6
Specific gravity: 4·90-5·30
Refractive index: opaque
Crystal system: hexagonal, rhombohedral, massive, dense fibrous or reniform
Colour: red or gunmetal to blued steel

Haematite, once a very popular gemstone, has almost disappeared from the market and is now used only to a limited degree in men's cuff-links and tie clasps.

Gemstone material is usually reniform, but the massive material can also be used provided it is sufficiently pure and compacted. Not a great deal of true gemstone quality material has been discovered in Rhodesia, but small quantities of true reniform or kidney ore material have been discovered in the iron deposits in the Gatooma area, possibly from the 'Yank' claims. Because of its comparative scarcity, however, most Rhodesian material is disposed of as specimens.

JADE

Hardness: 6-7
Specific gravity: 2·9-3·1
Refractive index: 1·60-1·64
Crystal system: monoclinic, granular, massive, tough and compact
Colour: white through yellow to dark green

Jade is an all-embracing term which covers a variety of minerals of a tough compact nature which have been used since prehistoric times for carving and producing items of adornment in addition to tools and weapons. The term should, however, be used only to describe the two main mineral species which form the true jade group—jadeite and nephrite.

Jadeite

A mineral of the pyroxene family which has been discovered only in Burma, China and Tibet and can be easily distinguished from the less valuable nephrite by a series of simple tests:

Jadeite fuses in a flame, nephrite is infusible:

Jadeite has a hardness of 6·5-7, while nephrite has a hardness of 6-6·5; it also has a higher specific gravity than nephrite.

Nephrite (Fig. 19, page 62)

Less valuable than jadeite, nephrite is a member of the amphibole family and has been located in many parts of the world. In appearance it is very similar to jadeite and it takes an excellent polish. It is therefore in great demand in the Far East for carving and ornamental work. Good material has been mined at Mashaba on the Prince chrome mine in association with the chrome and serpentine and it is possible that further deposits may be located in the vicinity of the Great Dyke and other serpentine bodies which abound in Rhodesia.

KYANITE (Figs. 20, 21, pages 62, 63)

Hardness: 4·5-7
Specific gravity: 3·56-3·67
Refractive index: 1·71-1·73
Crystal system: triclinic often in
    long blade-like crystals
Colour: colourless, blue (various
    shades) and brick

Kyanite is not a gemstone in the true sense of the word and good gem quality material is scarce. The stone is also unique because each crystal has two distinct hardnesses—4-4·5 with the grain and 7 across the grain. This quality makes the stone very hard to cut and consequently only a limited number of cut stones are located in various collections.

The material nevertheless makes a very handsome specimen and collectors will always welcome either single crystals, or clusters of the blade-like material, to display in prominent positions in their cabinets.

Fig. 12   Dumortierite

Fig. 13   Epidote

Fig. 14   Fluorspar

Fig. 15   Red amazonite, sunstone amazonite

Fig. 16   Unakite

Fig. 17   Garnet

Fig. 18   Haematite

Fig. 19   Nephrite jade

Fig. 20   Gem kyanite

Fig. 21   Kyanite

Fig. 22   Rose quartz

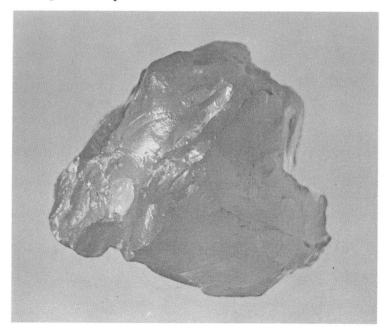

Fig. 23   Lepidolite and hiddenite

The material is fairly common in Rhodesia and is found in the pegmatites in the Urungwe, Fungwe and Mtoko areas. Clusters of crystals are frequently found embedded in the quartz.

In industry kyanite is used in the manufacture of refractory ware and also to toughen certain types of glass.

LEPIDOLITE (Fig. 23, page 64)
Hardness: 2·5-3
Specific gravity: 2·8-2·9
Refractive index: opaque
Crystal system: monoclinic
Colour: purple to reddish-purple

This is a mineral of the lithium group and not a true gemstone, being too soft to take and hold a good polish. It has, nevertheless, been used in dress rings and brooches and also as buttons. Its chief uses are in the industrial field in the manufacture of tough glass and porcelains. Lepidolite is the lightest known solid.

It is always found in association with the pegmatites, particularly in the Bikita area, where one of the world's largest deposits exists. However, both the Salisbury and Odzi areas contain deposits of importance.

MAGNESITE
Hardness: 4-4·5
Specific gravity: 3·0
Refractive index: opaque
Crystal system: massive, reniform and nodular
Colour: white

Magnesite is used in the manufacture of refractory bricks and linings of furnaces, not as a gemstone, but it can be carved and takes a fairly good polish. It can make an extremely interesting specimen and every now and again pieces resembling heads or animals can be located.

The most interesting material discovered in Rhodesia comes from the southern part of the country.

MARBLE (Fig. 5, page 36)
Hardness: 3·5-4
Specific gravity: 2·65-2·85
Refractive index: opaque

Crystal system: massive

Colour: white, brown, blue, black or a combination of all colours in blotches or streaks

Marble is a metamorphosed calcite or dolomite and is used extensively in the carving trade. Because of its comparative softness, it is reasonably easy to work and it takes an excellent polish.

It is fairly widespread throughout the world and Rhodesia, but the best quality local material from both the texture and colour points of view is to be found in the Sinoia and Urungwe areas.

OBSIDIAN

Hardness: 5-5·5

Specific gravity: 2·5-2·6

Refractive index: 1·5

Crystal system: massive

Colour: black to dark green

Obsidian, a glassy lava, has been used for a considerable time in the gem industry, being reasonably easy to work and capable of taking an excellent polish. It is often confused with pearlite, which is also a glassy lava having a slightly higher water content, but as far as the gem trade is concerned both materials are accepted under the common name obsidian.

The material occurs in fissures in the country rock, usually granite, and is fairly common in the south-eastern part of the country.

QUARTZ

This group of minerals is one of the most widespread in the world and produces, if not the most valuable, certainly the greatest variety of gemstones. It is, in fact, so vast and includes such a wide selection of gems, that it has been found necessary to break the main group down into three sub-groups and then each sub-group into anything up to ten classes of gemstones. Rhodesia has a large proportion of these various gemstones and one or other can be found in almost every corner of Rhodesia.

The three sub-groups are:

(1) *Massive* No crystal structure and is found in large or small amorphous masses.

(2) *Crystalline* This group normally develops in the hexagonal system, but may also be found in what appears to be the

massive form. This is not a mistake on the part of nature, but is caused by the later crystallization of the quartz following the faces of earlier crystallization.

(3) *Crypto-crystalline* This material has no visible crystal structure and normally appears to be amorphous. It is, however, usually made up of tightly packed minute fibrous bodies or crystals which cannot be detected by the naked eye.

Let us take each of the three groups separately:

Massive group
Hardness: 7·0
Specific gravity: 2·6-3·7
Refractive index: 1·54-1·55 (often opaque)
Crystal system: nil amorphous
Colour: various (depending on the gemstone)

Aventurine (Fig. 24, page 77)

Green (shades). Translucent to opaque. True aventurine quartz contains minute inclusions of mica which impart a sheen or schiller to the polished stone. Most Rhodesian material lacks these inclusions and is more aptly described as green quartz. Nevertheless, this material can be most attractive. The true material and the green quartz have been found in the Victoria district and are being exploited on a fairly large scale.

Milky quartz (Fig. 29, page 81)

A pale bluish-white material, vaguely translucent. Although not truly like moonstone (feldspar) it is sometimes mistaken for it, and has been erroneously marketed as 'Rhodesian moonstone'. When cut and polished or even tumbled, it makes a most attractive and unostentatious item of jewellery and can be worn with any colour. The material is fairly common and could be put to considerably more use than it is at present. The best quality stones are located in the Mtoko district, although it is possible that further sources of the material may be located in other parts of Rhodesia.

Rose quartz (Fig. 22, page 63)

Usually opaque to translucent. A popular semi-precious stone used in all forms of jewellery and ornamental work. Rhodesian material which has been produced to date seldom attains the standard required by the world market, being too pale and fractured. It is possible, however, that better material will be located in the Miami and Mtoko districts.

Tiger's eye (Fig. 25, page 78)
A form of silicified crocidolite asbestos which is common in certain parts of South Africa. It comes in a variety of colours from brown and gold to red or blue and has been reported from various sources in Rhodesia such as Shabani and Que Que. The authorities are, however, a little sceptical regarding these claims because no material has ever been found *in situ* and it is possible that rocks consisting of an intergrowth of quartz and felspar, which also have a chatoyant effect, are being mistakenly identified as tiger's eye by rockhounds. Recently, however, the author did have the opportunity to examine a piece of golden tiger's eye which had been discovered by a well known Rhodesian geologist. The material was not cuttable, being badly fractured, but it is another first which could lead to further interesting discoveries.

Crystalline group
The crystalline group has the following distinguishing properties:
Hardness: 7·0
Specific gravity: 2·64-2·69
Refractive index: 1·54-1·55
Crystal system: hexagonal
Colour: varied according to the
type of stone

The crystalline group contains the undermentioned stones:

Amethyst (Fig. 27, page 79)
This is one of the commonest but nevertheless still one of the most popular gemstones in the world. The colour range varies from a pale violet purple to a deep almost opaque purple, occasionally showing tinges of red. This latter colour is most common in Brazilian stones and has not yet been located in Rhodesia.
The crystals are found either in geodes or clusters and occasionally as single, doubly terminated crystals. These doubly terminated crystals not only produce perfect stones but also make

excellent specimens and, unless the rockhound is fortunate enough to secure several specimens, the tendency is to retain the specimen at the expense of a beautiful stone.

Good quality material has been discovered in both the pegmatites and the basalts in the Beitbridge, Featherstone, Mtoko, Urungwe and Wankie areas, but only the Mtoko area has produced the doubly terminated single crystals.

Citrine (Fig. 28, page 80)

A pale golden yellow to deep golden brown quartz which can make a very pleasing gemstone, citrine is frequently mounted in brooches and rings. Poor quality amethyst is sometimes burnt to give the stone a deep rich golden brown colour and this material is often confused with citrine or golden topaz. Amethyst, however, normally has a lamellar structure which is not known in citrine or topaz and is therefore readily distinguished.

Citrine of good quality has been located in the Marandellas/Wedza area and also to a lesser extent in Miami. It is always associated with the pegmatites.

Rock crystal

This is a clear, colourless quartz common throughout Rhodesia in crystals ranging from match head size to desk size. It has a wide variety of uses ranging from jewellery and carving to optical instruments, glass manufacture and radio parts. It is a popular collector's piece either as single doubly terminated crystals or in small clusters of well shaped crystals.

The crystals frequently contain inclusions of other material such as rutile, tourmaline, actinolite and even whole amethyst crystals. The material which contains inclusions is very popular in the jewellery and carving industries. Good specimens are also in great demand by collectors.

It is normally associated with pegmatites and is very widespread throughout Rhodesia.

Smoky quartz or cairngorm (Fig. 29, page 81)

Cairngorm, which is nothing more than smoky quartz of a slightly different shade, that is yellow to brown as opposed to the grey of smoky quartz, is usually associated with Scotland, but is, in fact, found almost anywhere that smoky quartz is found.

A fairly popular gemstone or specimen when in small clean crystals. Fair to good quality material has been found in the Urungwe and Marandellas areas, while deposits of lesser grade material are known in the Mtoko and Victoria districts.

The dark, almost opaque material which has little value, is sometimes known as morion.

Cryptocrystalline group

The cryptocrystalline group, which contains a vast amount of gemstone material, has the following characteristics:

Hardness: 7·0

Specific gravity: 2·5–2·8

Refractive index: 1·54–1·55

Crystal system: usually amorphous in appearance, but comprised of tightly packed minute radiating fibres or crystals

Colour: varies with the type of material

Agate (Fig. 26, page 78)

The agate is the commonest but, at the same time, one of the most popular materials used by jewellers, carvers, collectors and rockhounds. The cut and polished stone has a high lustre and polish which is seldom matched by other stones and the wide variety of patterns and colours in which it is found make it a wonderful collector's item. Americans, in particular, are great enthusiasts in this field and some collections are quite bewildering in their range of colours and types.

As a rule certain areas are noted for a particular variety of agate, but frequently in gravel beds and major rivers we find a very wide variety of stones which have been carried there by storm water from many different sources. The true source of agate in Rhodesia is, however, the basalts which occur in such places as Bumi Hills, Featherstone, lower Sabi and Matibi, Tuli, Mafunga-busi, Tjolotjo and Wankie. Alluvial sources are the Sebakwe, Umniati, Ngezi, Sabi, Gwaai, Limpopo and Zambezi rivers.

The most common form of agate is the banded agate in two or more colours, but in addition to this type, we have 'moss' agate which has green, brown and reddish moss-like inclusions; 'tree' agate with dendritic-like trees, bushes or fern-shaped inclusions; 'picture' agate with various coloured markings, making very pleasant land and seascape pictures, and 'lace' agate with uniform bands of white inclusions which produce a lacey effect in the cut stone. In addition to the varieties already named, black and white banded agate is known as 'onyx' while red and white, or brown and white banded material is known as 'sardonyx'.

Chalcedony (Figs. 26, 30, pages 78, 82)

Chalcedony ranges in colour from white through grey to blue and also green. It is usually opaque to semi-translucent and can be found in most agate beds. White and grey are the most common and are of little or no use as gemstones. A variety of the white, which has formed small rose-like growths (known as beekites) often surrounded by small quartz crystals, make interesting collector's pieces. This material is fairly common in the Featherstone area. Good blue chalcedony is not common in Rhodesia, the best quality being obtained from South West Africa, but small quantities of a light blue have, nevertheless, been discovered in the Tjolotjo and Bumi districts. Green chalcedony or 'mtorolite' as it is now called, has been discovered in two or three different places along the northern end of the Great Dyke and Umtali. The material is unique to Rhodesia, being the only deposit in the world of good chalcedony which is naturally deep emerald green. The green coloration is due to the presence of chromium and it is very popular as a gemstone or a collector's item.

Carnelian

Carnelian is a translucent material, red, brown or yellow in colour. It cuts well and takes an excellent polish and is consequently a fairly popular gemstone. These stones are usually found in agate beds but, like agate, can also be located in certain rivers.

Chrysoprase (Fig. 28, page 80)

An apple green form of chalcedony, much lighter in colour than mtorolite, has been discovered in several areas in Rhodesia, but the best quality material to reach the market came from the Eastern Districts. Our local stones fall far short of the top Australian grade, but nevertheless it has been established that deposits exist and better quality is bound to come to light in the future.

Unlike mtorolite which is coloured by chromium, chrysoprase owes its apple green colour to the presence of nickel hydroxide.

Jasper (Fig. 32, page 83)

Jasper is found in reds, browns and greens or combinations of both green and red. The green material which is flecked with red is known as heliotrope or bloodstone and is fairly popular as a gemstone. The colouring is due to ferric oxide. Jasper is usually found in association with agate and chalcedony.

Opalite (Dyke opal) (Fig. 31, page 82)

Opal, although one of the silica (quartz) group, differs to such an extent from all other members of the group that it is best recorded as a separate item.

Hardness: 5-6·5
Specific gravity: 2·0
Refractive index: 1·44-1·46
Crystal system: amorphous
Colour: white, blue-green, brown and pink frequently mixed together in the same stone

The material which varies from opaque to translucent is very brittle and consequently hard to cut. If, however, anyone is successful in his endeavours to cut a well coloured translucent stone, his labours are well rewarded. Opalite differs considerably from the true opal which is mined in Australia and Mexico, and although it is basically the same material, it lacks the iridescent display of colours contained in the Australian material and the red fire of the Mexican material.

The stone is located on and adjacent to the Great Dyke and is also in the alluvial beds of streams which rise on the Dyke.

SERPENTINE (Fig. 33, page 84)

Hardness: 3-4
Specific gravity: 2·5-2·7
Refractive index: opaque
Crystal system: monoclinic, often compact and massive
Colour: green, greenish-yellow, sometimes mottled with whites and reds

Being a comparatively soft stone, it is seldom used in the gem trade, although when the colour is right it can be used in brooches and necklaces. However, the more common use is in the carving trade. Certain varieties of the more compacted material take an excellent polish. This applies particularly to a beautiful deep green material which has been discovered in the Sinoia area. Unfortunately, this material is scarce and not easily mined, hence very little ever finds it way on to the market.

Recently another variety of green serpentine was discovered in the Gwelo area. The material is traversed by thin veins of quartz and carbonate substance and also includes minute specks of what appear to be chalcopyrite, which gives the cut stone a very interesting appearance.

Serpentine is common along the Great Dyke, Victoria, Belingwe, Que Que and certain parts of the Eastern Districts.

Bowenite

This is a member of the serpentine family also known as 'Noble Serpentine'. In appearance it is usually translucent green to yellow-green and can be confused with nephrite jade. But because of its hardness, 3-4 as opposed to jade's 5-6 a quick scratch test will banish any doubts.

It has been found in the Mashaba area and also to a lesser extent in the Odzi district.

Bowenite has a refractive index of 1·49-1·57.

SCAPOLITE
    Hardness: 5-6
    Specific gravity: 2·54-2·77
    Refractive index: 1·55-1·57
    Crystal system: tetragonal
    Colour: colourless, sometimes
      pale pink

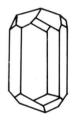

Scapolite is not well known as a gemstone. It is too soft to withstand much use and that fact, combined with its pale colour and rather low refractive index, tends to put off the average buyer of gems. In its pink form it has been known to exhibit a very strong chatoyancy which, when cut, produces a remarkably clear cat's eye. As far as is known, this type of material has not been located in Rhodesia. It is possible, however, that it may be found in some of the larger pegmatites.

Finds of scapolite have been recorded from the Miami, Karoi and Urungwe areas. It always appears to be associated with pegmatites and will no doubt be found in other localities before long.

SPHENE

Hardness: 5·5
Specific gravity: 3·53
Refractive index: 1·90-2·03
Crystal system: monoclinic
Colour: yellow, brown and green

Sphene is one of the more uncommon minerals which interest collectors and is seldom used as a ring stone because of its comparative softness. It is nevertheless much sought after as a collector's piece. It can and often is confused with zircon because of its colour and high refractive index. However, this is where the similarity ends. Zircon has a hardness of 7·5 against sphene's 5·5 and the specific gravity of zircon is much higher at 4·4-4·7 while sphene is only 3·53.

Another interesting factor is that sphene is strongly pleochroic and will exhibit two totally different colours when viewed from different angles.

Sphene is usually found in pegmatites in association with albite and hornblende and has been reported from the Miami/Chirundu areas where it occurs in small crystals. As far as is known, no big crystal or cuttable material has, as yet, been located in Rhodesia.

SOAPSTONE (Talc)

Hardness: 1-2
Specific gravity: 2·7-2·8
Refractive index: 1·54-1·59
Crystal system: orthorhombic, monoclinic or massive
Colour: pale green, yellow-green and brown, usually a combination of all three colours

Because of its comparative softness, soapstone can never be classed as a gemstone. It can neither take a good polish nor hold for long what little polish it does take. It is therefore totally unsuited for anything other than carving of figurines and other ornaments. The carved material is more often than not treated with oil to give it a slight sheen and to assist in preserving the stone. It is a very popular medium for African carvers whose work in this sphere is in fairly high demand in Europe and America.

The best known deposits are situated in the Inyanga area, while lesser deposits are also found at Fort Victoria and Que Que and a beautiful pale translucent green material is occasionally produced from the Selukwe chrome mines.

SODALITE (Fig. 35, page 85)
Hardness: 5-6
Specific gravity: 2·2-2·4
Refractive index: 1·48
Crystal system: cubic, massive and compact
Colour: grey to blue mottled with white

This material is a little on the soft side for a true gemstone, but can be used for items such as brooches. Its true value lies in the ease with which it can be carved and polished and many beautiful *objets d'art* have come off the carver's bench.

Top quality material is scarce in Rhodesia, but some fairly good light blue stones have been mined in the Miami/Urungwe areas.

SPINEL
Hardness: 8
Specific gravity: 3·5-4·1
Refractive index: 1·72
Crystal system: cubic
Colour: red, brown and black

Spinel is a well known gemstone in the Far East, particularly in Ceylon, Burma and Siam, but it is also found to a lesser extent in Brazil and the U.S.A. The material is excellent for cutting and takes a wonderful polish.

Small crystals—rather dark in colour, have been reported from the pegmatites in the Miami and Odzi areas, but as far as can be ascertained, no true gem quality material has, as yet, been located in Rhodesia, and it is most unlikely that any stones have been cut from the local material.

SPODUMENE (Fig. 23, page 64)
Hardness: 6·5-7
Specific gravity: 3·2
Refractive index: 1·66-1·67
Crystal system: monoclinic
Colour: pink—kunzite, yellow
to green—hiddenite and opaque purple

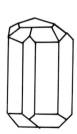

Good quality kunzite and hiddenite are very rare and hence one is not likely to see cut gemstones for sale in the usual jeweller's shop. All the better stones have long since found their way into the important collections of the world and are only on display once in a while. To the average man in the street, a good quality spodumene would pass almost unnoticed. It may have a slightly higher refractive index than beryl or tourmaline, but it can in no way match the depth of colour that is found in these stones. It is therefore unlikely to become a truly popular gemstone.

Rhodesia has vast deposits of spodumene but, so far as is known, the only gem material ever to be recovered from one of these deposits is a small yellowish piece of hiddenite which is reputed to have been discovered by chance in the Salisbury district. It is possible, however, that if the pegmatites in the Salisbury and Bikita areas were subjected to a closer examination, more of the material would come to light.

The common form of spodumene—opaque purple material—is fairly common and when sufficiently compacted can produce a very interesting cabochon.

STAUROLITE (Fig. 36, page 86)

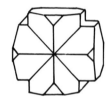

Hardness: 7
Specific gravity: 3·8
Refractive index: 1·73-1·74
Crystal system: orthorhombic
Colour: brown to black

Staurolite, a mineral associated with high grade metamorphosed rocks, is found in the Urungwe area and also as an alluvial deposit in the small stream beds which drain down into the Zambezi Valley east of Chirundu.

The stone is usually opaque but is also found as a translucent deep honey brown material which can be cut into attractive gemstones. Twinning of the crystals is very common and well formed staurolite crosses or 'Fairy crosses' are common. The crosses are frequently worn as pendants and used to be regarded as good luck charms.

Fig. 24   Aventurine

Fig. 25 Golden tiger's eye

Fig. 26 Agate and chalcedony

Fig. 27   Amethyst

Fig. 28 Chrysoprase and citrine

Fig. 29   Smoky quartz and milky quartz

Fig. 30   Mtorolite

Fig. 31   Opalite

Fig. 32   Red jasper

Fig. 33   Serpentine

Fig. 34   Thulite

Fig. 35   Sodalite

Fig. 36 Staurolite

Fig. 37   Topaz

Fig. 38   Tourmalines

Fig. 39   Wood opal

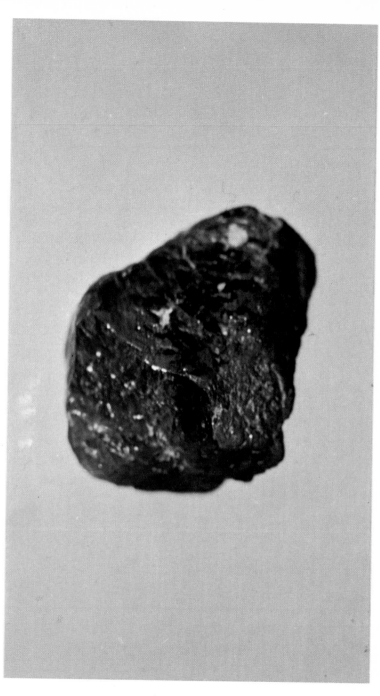

Fig. 40   Zircon

Fig. 41 Cabochons

Fig. 42   Faceted stones

THULITE (Zoisite family) (Fig. 34, page 84)
 Hardness: 6-6·5
 Specific gravity: 3·45-3·48
 Refractive index: opaque
 Crystal system: orthorhombic and massive
 Colour: rose red, usually appearing as blobs of colour in a
   greenish-grey host rock (epidote) or as flecks in jade

A fairly attractive stone which can be carved or cabochoned
and takes a good polish. It is not in great demand because of the
large variety of better known materials which are currently
available.

The only known source of reasonably good material is Mashaba, but it is possible that it could also occur in the Odzi area.

TOPAZ (Fig. 37, page 87)
 Hardness: 8
 Specific gravity: 3·5-3·58
 Refractive index: 1·6-1·63
 Crystal system: orthorhombic
 Colour: colourless, blue, golden,
   green or red

Topaz is a very popular gemstone which is equally prized by
the collector and person who is fortunate enough to possess a piece
of jewellery containing the stone.

Crystals are fairly common because the stone is often found in
a kaolin type of material which has protected it from the stresses
and strains to which the pegmatites have been subjected.

Rhodesia is very fortunate in being able to claim at least one
deposit of good quality blue (Miami district) and several deposits
of colourless material in the same vicinity. No golden, green or
red stones have, however, been located in Rhodesia, but like
everything else in this young country, there is no knowing what
will be found tomorrow.

TOURMALINE (Fig. 38, page 88)
 Hardness: 7
 Specific gravity: 3·05-3·12
 Refractive index: 1·62-1·64
 Crystal system: hexagonal, often

in slightly curved three-sided
crystals
Colour: green—tourmaline
        red—rubellite
        blue—indicolite
        brown—dravite
        black—schorl
        also colourless and yellow

Possibly tourmaline has a greater variety of colours than any other known gemstone as can be seen from the list above. Tourmaline is one of the few stones which will combine several of its colours in one crystal. The most common combination is known as the 'water melon' variety which contains a core of red (rubelite) surrounded by a thin skin of colourless tourmaline which in turn is encased in a skin of bright green. This material is seldom of good cutting quality, but makes a most attractive ornament when sliced at right angles to the 'c' axis and polished.

Combinations of colours (red and green or blue and brown) often occur in the crystal, one above the other, and can be cut to display either or both colours.

Good quality material has been located in the Miami, Urungwe and Fungwe areas in association with the pegmatites.

WOOD OPAL (Fig. 39, page 89)
    Hardness: 5·5-6
    Specific gravity: 2·00-2·48
    Refractive index: opaque
    Crystal system: nil
    Colour: usually red, green and brown in various shades

Wood opal or petrified, fossilized or silicified wood should really be included in the quartz group of gemstones, but it is not normally accepted as being a true mineral and is frequently protected as a national relic in countries where it is scarce.

Ancient forests which became immersed in water containing silica are the basis of petrified wood. The decaying cells of the wood were gradually replaced by the silica and, because each growth ring in any particular tree varies in hardness, decay seems to have taken place at varying rates. The replacement by the silica has been at different times with the result that the wood opal has several different colours showing in the same stone.

Much of the wood opal found in Rhodesia is badly fractured and cannot be used in the gemstone trade, but certain deposits situated in the vicinity of the Mafungabusi Plateau and the Zambesi Valley, not only have excellent colour but are relatively free from cracks and inclusions and some first class material has been located there.

ZIRCON (Fig. 40, page 90)
    Hardness: 7·5
    Specific gravity: 4·4-4·7
    Refractive index: 1·92-1·98
    Crystal system: tetragonal
    Colour: brown, blue, green, red
      or colourless

Small zircons have been located in Rhodesia and at one time a block of claims was registered for zirconium in the Umtali area. According to the records, no cuttable material has been produced. It is possible, however, that something worthwhile will come to light one of these days.

Zircon is a beautiful gemstone when clear and bright and has a brilliance second only to the diamond.

Synthetic and Imitation Stones

The manufacture of synthetic stones is a fast growing and obviously lucrative business and jewellery containing these man-made stones can be found in almost any jeweller's shop. A display of these synthetic stones is truly magnificent, because the size and brilliance of the average synthetic exceeds that of any natural stone which is likely to be owned by the average man in the street. Because of the size and perfection of these stones, they can usually be distinguished from the natural stone and the purchase price is usually considerably less than the amount one would expect to pay for the genuine article.

The most common materials used in the production of synthetics are corundum and spinel. With these two components and the addition of various colouring agents such as chromium, alumina, iron and titanium, various synthetic stones from ruby and sapphire to aquamarine and alexandrite can be produced. In addition to these stones, synthetic emeralds are now manufactured in America, France and Germany and usually emerald material is used to produce the synthetic stone.

Synthetic rutile is also produced in America and Europe and, although rutile in the natural state is not classed as a gemstone, the synthetic stone has a brilliance which far exceeds that of a diamond. It is a truly superb stone when cut, usually clear with a faint yellow tinge, but it is also found in reds and blues. Unfortunately, it is fairly soft, 6 to 6·5, and is therefore seldom used as a ring stone. Another synthetic which can match a diamond for brilliance is strontium titanate, but again, unfortunately, or possibly fortunately, this stone is also fairly soft, approximately 5·5 on the Mohs' scale.

Diamonds and quartz are also produced synthetically and are used commercially—diamonds in tools and cutting heads and quartz in various industries associated with radio and electronics.

The processes by which these synthetics are produced are usually a closely guarded secret of the manufacturers but, basically, extremely high temperatures and pressure are required to grow the boules from which these gemstones are cut. Possibly the best known equipment used in the manufacture of these boules is the Verneuil furnace which has been perfected in America. There are no doubt other systems in use which may work equally well, but very little appears to have been written about them.

It is often very difficult to detect a well made synthetic stone and if any doubt exists in the minds of the reader regarding the genuineness of a particular stone, he should not hesitate to have it tested by an expert.

However, a few basic tests indicated below may assist in arriving at an accurate assessment of the stone's genuineness.

Corundum

1   The colour in synthetic rubies and sapphires is often a guide; it usually has the appearance of being too gaudy or bright.
2   Bubbles of gas or liquid are often present in synthetic corundum. The bubbles, often present in considerable numbers, can be readily detected through a good hand lens.
3   Synthetic corundum always shows curved growth lines due to the fairly rapid growth of the boule. The natural stone's growth lines are always straight.

Spinel

These stones, like corundum, also contain bubbles, though less in number and the growth lines in some stones show a fairly marked curve. The stones are, however, extremely difficult to detect.

Emerald

Like spinel, this is very difficult to detect, but can sometimes be detected by the colour or by specific gravity tests. Natural emerald has a specific gravity of 2·71 while the synthetic stone never seems to exceed 2·65.

Imitation stones are usually fairly easy to detect, being made from glass or paste. These stones always lack lustre and dispersion. Because they are made from glass, they scratch fairly easily and old stones always look dull. The stones can also be scratched by a file, but possibly the most effective test is the feel of the stone. Natural stones which have not been handled immediately prior to the test being carried out, feel cool to the touch; glass on the other hand has a warm feel.

Inclusions in Gemstones and other rocks

Gemstones in their natural state often contain inclusions of other minerals. In certain stones this can be used as a means of identifying the source of the stone or possibly a means of proving its genuineness. One of the outstanding examples of this can be found in the Sandawana emerald which contains a vast quantity of minute tremolite needles criss-crossing each other without any set pattern. These needles are only found in the Sandawana stones and are positive identification, not only of a genuine emerald but of the exact locality from which it was produced. These inclusions are, however, microscopic. They can only be detected with the use of a fairly powerful microscope and are therefore of no particular interest to the average rockhound.

Inclusions which are visible to the naked eye, such as rutile hairs in quartz, actinolite needles forming a regular radiating pattern as found in quartz or small dark tourmaline crystals are of more interest to the amateur because they can readily be seen and appreciated whitout the use of special equipment.

Other inclusions of interest are the small specks of chrome which are found in the nephrite jade from Mashaba, and the bubbles of moisture sometimes found in amethyst crystal. Picture, lace or moss agate depend for their beauty on the inclusions which have made a dull stone into a colourful and interesting one. Other inclusions which are of interest to the rockhound are the minute crystalline rods which are found in cat's eye chrysoberyl or the 'silk' such as that found in apatite, corundum or quartz which enables one to cut 'eye' or 'star' stones.

In certain limestones, shales and sandstones, fossil remains of once living creatures, organisms or plant life can be found. These are of tremendous interest not only to the rockhound but also to the geologist who can date the rock formation from the type of fossil which it contains.

Inclusions in gemstones can be placed in three clear cut and well defined categories:

1   Pre-existing inclusions—those which were present as fully grown or formed material prior to the crystallization of the second substance.

2   Contemporaneous inclusions—those which formed within the main rock, at the same time that crystallization of the surrounding mass was taking place.

3   Subsequent inclusions—following crystallization of any particular mineral, movement in the earth's surface often caused cracks to appear in the solid. At some later date these cracks were filled with other substances which in turn crystallized.

The substances which can form inclusions are:

1   Gaseous substance which occurs as bubbles either with or without liquid in the crystal.

2   Liquid inclusions which appear as small bubbles containing liquid and which can be readily detected.

3   Solid inclusions such as fibres or small well formed crystals which can frequently be seen with the naked eye and are more often than not totally different in composition to the host rock.

Gaseous and liquid inclusions often form what is referred to in the gem trade as 'snow'. These inclusions are common in beryls and detract considerably from the value of the stone. Solid inclusions seldom detract from the value. In fact, they more often than not enhance the value of the crystal from a collector's point of view.

Cutting and polishing Gemstones

For the lover of beautiful things a well cut and polished gemstone must be the supreme example of and the ultimate in beauty. There are very few people who are not attracted by a display of gemstones. The colour and sparkle of cut stones is unsurpassed by anything else known to man.

Long before man left for posterity any written evidence of his advancing civilization, he was cutting, carving and polishing gemstones. His first attempts were possibly nothing more than rubbing one stone against another, which means that only very soft materials such as soapstone would have been used in those days.

Gradually man developed crude machines to assist in his cutting and with these machines came the breakthrough on grinding and polishing grits. The ancient Chinese were possibly the first in this field, using orange sticks dipped in corundum or garnet dust to produce those superb jade carvings. These objects of beauty took years to complete and, in certain cases, a son would finish off work started by his father.

The first crude machines used only human power to turn the lap. A refinement of this machine with a treadle to produce movement can be seen to this day in the cottage industries of India, Ceylon, Burma and China. These cutters have grown up in the business. The secrets of cutting and polishing have been handed down from father to son and are jealously guarded by the family. It is doubtful if they would even thank you for one of the modern amateur electrically powered machines with its chromium plated adjustable faceting head. Such professional cutters prefer the jam peg type of equipment with a lap speed that they can control automatically by their feet or hand movements.

It will not be possible to cover all aspects of cutting and polishing in this chapter, but a short examination of the various processes employed by cutters may be of assistance to the amateur.

VARIOUS CUTS IN COMMON USE

Cabochon

Emerald Cut

Step Cut

Step Cut Oval

Step Cushion Cut

Brilliant

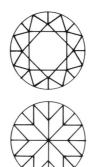

Marquise

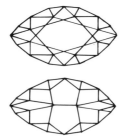

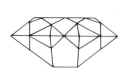

Pendeloque

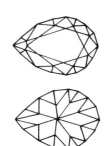

Diamond saw

The most important single item of equipment for anyone wishing to embark on this hobby is a diamond saw. With this device the cutter can slab large lumps of material, thereby getting the most out of his rough. He can preform his stones and in so doing, save time and labour on the actual shaping and polishing.

The machine in itself is remarkably simple, the most expensive items being the blade and the motor. This latter item can, however, be hooked up to other equipment when not being used to drive the saw. There are several models available to the amateur, but the best results from an all purpose saw will be achieved from a twenty centimetre diameter blade of medium thickness. With care this blade can be used to slab material up to ten centimetres in thickness as well as doing the more finicky work of preforming the slabs before grinding.

The saw must, however, be treated with care and respect in order to obtain the best results and a few tips on care and maintenance will never be wasted.

1 Blade manufacturers usually specify the most suitable speed at which to run the blade and this should be observed as nearly as possible provided that the speed is not such that the machine develops vibrations and chatter.

2 The machine housing should be of fairly heavy and robust construction and be securely fastened to a heavy workbench. This will tend to lessen vibrations which would otherwise make accurate work impossible.

3 The blade should under no circumstances be used dry. It must always run in a bath of lubricant or coolant, sufficient in depth to cover at least the bottom centimetre of the blade when it is at rest. The best lubricant or coolant is kerosene or a mixture of kerosene and oil, although certain manufacturers may recommend other liquids.

4 Many cutters, particularly the professionals, scorn the use of a clamp and guides to ensure that the stone which is being cut runs true in the same plane and direction, but unless one is an expert, the best guarantee you can get to ruin a blade is to feed the stone through by hand. The use of clamps and guide rails is therefore recommended.

5 When feeding the stone through the saw, particular care must be taken to ensure that the stone goes through at a

steady pressure. This pressure must be controlled and at no time be so great as to cause the saw blade to buck and slow down or become heated.

6 When you have finished your cutting for the day, clean the blade, the clamp and the saw platform and always leave it in as spotless a condition as possible. This will not only help to preserve the saw, but will enable you to get on with the next lot of sawing without any delay.

Cutting and polishing

Because this is such a vast subject in itself and because there are so many excellent books covering every aspect of cutting available on the market today, it is not intended to do more than touch very superficially on the business of cutting and polishing. It is, however, strongly recommended to those people who wish to take up this hobby, but are unable to obtain tuition from an experienced cutter or gem society, that they obtain through their local bookshop one of the better books on cutting, such as:

Gemcraft by LELANDE QUICK and HUGH LEIPER, or

Gem Cutting by JOHN SINKANKAS.

Gem cutting can, for all practical purposes, be divided into four categories:

1 Tumbling
2 Carving
3 Cabochoning
4 Faceting

Tumbling

Tumbling, as the name implies, is the grinding and polishing of stones by the action of the stones rubbing one against the other, in much the same way that agates, retrieved from a riverbed often show indications of a rough polish. Tumbling today is undertaken by most cutters who find amongst their normal cutting materials a fairly big proportion of rough which cannot be cabochoned or faceted and rather than discard it, they place the material in a revolving drum to which various abrasives and polishing agents in the form of a sludge or slurry are added. Tumbling is a long and time consuming process, but fortunately, does not require very much attention other than a quick examination once a day.

Points worth remembering when tumbling are:

(*a*) Always use stones which have approximately the same hardness and toughness. Do not for instance, put agate and sodalite in the same tumbler, otherwise you will find the sodalite has disappeared when you open the drum.

(*b*) Endeavour to keep all stones in any one run to approximately the same size and, if possible, preform the stones so that the finished product will be more or less standard in shape and size.

(*c*) Always ensure that the tumbler and the stones are thoroughly cleaned before introducing a new and finer abrasive or polishing agent.

(*d*) Ensure that the breather hole is always clear otherwise the drum may explode.

Carving

Carving is a hobby which has always attracted the more artistic element of the human race, and it is possible that man's first venture into the field of shaping stones was, in fact, crude carvings such as a flint axe or arrow heads, cutting and skinning knives and even carved outlines of animals in caves.

Gradually these crude carvings gave place to items of adornment and household and religious utensils, examples of which have been recovered in China and Mexico. The stone most favoured for carving has always been jade or jadeite and some magnificent examples of this ancient work can be viewed in the great collections in various parts of the world today.

The ancient Chinese used orange sticks dipped in corundum powder and twirled between the fingers or the palms of the hands for their early carvings. This method gradually gave way to the bow and free turning drill stick and in our modern age we have introduced an electric motor driving a cutting tool through a flexible cable. The basic method of cutting and polishing is, however, unchanged from those early Chinese methods.

In place of the orange stick dipped in corundum, we now have small abrasive wheels or discs and corundum- or diamond-tipped tools. In addition, various other refinements which, although allowing us to finish the carving in considerably less time, do not improve on the line and beauty of these ancient carvings.

Materials commonly used for carving range from the soft

soapstone through sodalite, the jades to quartz and occasionally corundum, but the favourite stone is still jade because the beautiful polish and finish that this stone can take is superior to that taken by any other stone.

Anyone wishing to try their hand at carving should start with soapstone and advance slowly through the softer materials before tackling the tougher stones. Carving soapstone or magnesite requires nothing more than a pocket knife, a file, fine emery paper and a fair amount of patience.

Cabochoning

Cabochon equipment is relatively simple and although there are many cabbing units on the market, those people who are capable of and enjoy making things will have no difficulty in knocking together a serviceable unit.

The most common units are those which have the grinding wheels running in the vertical position, although horizontal laps are also available, but provided the equipment is looked after, the vertical running machine is all that the amateur need ever require. The unit should consist of two grinding wheels, one to do the rough shaping, say 100 grit, and one of approximately 220 grit to do the final shaping and smooth away the deeper scores. In addition to the grinding wheels a sander for the final smoothing of the stone and a buffing wheel to impart the final polish are also essentials. All four wheels can be housed on the same machine but, if this is done, care must be taken to ensure that the buffing wheel never gets contaminated by grit flying off the grinding wheels, otherwise the finished stone will always have scratches on the surface.

The grinding wheels should never be used dry and possibly the easiest method of keeping them damp is to fix a sponge in the drip tray in such a manner that it is always in contact with the wheel when it is running. It is essential, however, to ensure that the grinding wheels are not allowed to remain in contact with water when the machine is not in use because, not only will this ruin the wheel, but it will also cause a throwing action on the wheel which will upset the balance of the whole machine and make good cutting almost impossible.

When grinding, the whole face of the wheel should be used, otherwise it will wear unevenly and prevent the cutter from obtaining the perfect cut stone. Finally, no matter how careful the operator is, the wheels will always tend to develop ridges and bumps and care must be taken to trim the wheel as often as is necessary with a diamond tipped tool, thereby ensuring that the best possible stones are produced.

Faceting

Faceting equipment has remained basically unchanged in principle since man first started polishing flat surfaces on stones. In other words, there has always been a revolving lap impregnated with a grinding powder. As far as can be determined, the lap has always revolved in the horizontal position and can be made of any substance which will allow the grit to become embedded in the surface. The method of propulsion has, however, gradually changed over from manually rotated to electrically driven equipment, although many of the true professional cutters still favour the manually driven lap, because this enables them to vary the speed during cutting and polishing, a refinement which cannot be achieved on electrically powered machines.

Possibly the greatest advance in faceting equipment is to be found in the actual facet head which is now available to the amateur. This head can be set at any angle and, provided care is taken by the cutter, the finished stone will always be symmetrical.

Glossary of common terms used in geology and gemmology

Adamantine	having a diamond-like lustre.
Adit	a horizontal tunnel, usually at the base of a cliff or hill, through which entry can be made into a mine.
Banded	rock formed by various layers of mineral substances such as agate and banded iron-stone.
Basalt	a dark, almost black, fine-grained extrusive rock.
Bedrock	solid rock underlying gravels, sand or clay.
Beekite	a concretionary deposit of minerals such as calcite and chalcedony, forming rosette-like stone shapes.
Biaxial	a crystal having two optic axes giving no double refraction.
Biotite	one of the mica group minerals, dark brown to green in colour and a frequent host to gemstone crystals such as beryls and garnets.
Birefringence	double refraction in crystals caused by the splitting of light beams into two and the different velocity at which the beams travel.
Blue ground	the slatey blue ground which forms the diamond-bearing kimberlite.
Bort	gemstone material which is too small, dirty and fractured to be of value to the gem trade.
Botryoidal	having the form of a bunch of grapes, for example, haematite.
Brachy axis	the shorter lateral axis in orthorhombic and triclinic crystals.
Carat	has two meanings. In respect of gemstones, it refers to mass, 1 carat = one-fifth of a

	gram. In respect of gold it refers to the purity or fineness of the metal, pure gold being 24 carats.
Chatoyance	the lustre in certain semi-opaque stones which resembles the changing lustres in the eye of a cat.
Cleavage	the tendency in crystals to split along pre-determined planes.
Conchoidal fracture	a curved fracture as seen in flints and quartz.
Conglomerate	fragments of rock, usually rounded and water worn cemented together by another mineral.
Contact	the point where two different rocks come together.
Crown	the upper part of a cut gemstone.
Cryptocrystalline	crystalline formation, but so small that it cannot be detected even with a good lens.
Crystalline	belonging to one of the recognized crystal groups.
Dendrite	crystallization of a mineral in the form of a tree on or in another mineral.
Druse	a lining of crystals inside a cavity.
Etching	roughened markings on a crystal face.
Facet	polished face of a gemstone.
Fluorescence	glow given off by certain minerals under ultra-violet light.
Fracture	the manner and appearance of a mineral when broken.
Geode	hollow rock formations usually containing crystals projecting into the hollow centre. Normally spherical in shape.
Girdle	that part of a cut gemstone which divides the crown from the pavilion.
Greasy	when applied to minerals, indicates the oily lustre of the mineral.
Hackly	jagged, pointed fracture.
Hardness	the ability of a stone to resist scratching.
Heavy liquids	a group of organic liquids used for determining the specific gravity of certain minerals.

Inclusion	crystals or fragments of minerals or other substances which have been enclosed in larger crystals.
Interfacial angle	the angle between faces on a crystal.
Kimberlite	see also blue ground. The volcanic rock found in pipes, which could and often does contain diamonds.
Lap	a flat disc impregnated with diamond or corundum powder, used for cutting and polishing gemstones.
Lustre	the light reflected from the surface of minerals.
Massive	amorphous, homogeneous mass of mineral substance.
Opalescence	the milky reflection seen in the interior of some minerals.
Pavilion	the portion of a cut gemstone which is below the girdle.
Pegmatite	coarse-grained dyke-like body consisting basically of granite and feldspar and containing such minerals as beryl, mica, garnet, tin quartz, tantalite, etc.
Pleochroism	the differential absorption of light by certain minerals which change colour when rotated.
Schiller	metallic-like lustre or iridescence contained in certain minerals.
Streak	the powder deposit left on a streak plate when a mineral is drawn across it.
Streak plate	usually an unglazed porcelain tablet used for testing the streak.
Twin, twinned	a non-parallel intergrowth of two or more crystals.
Vug	a cavity in a rocky formation usually containing a lining of a mineral which differs from the surrounding rock.